PRODUCT ESTHETICS

ZDZISLAW MARIAN LEWALSKI

PRODUCT ESTHETICS

AN INTERPRETATION FOR DESIGNERS

Design & Development Engineering Press
Carson City, Nevada

Library of Congress Cataloging in Publication Data

Lewalski, Zdzislaw M. (Zdzislaw Marian), 1934-
    Product esthetics.

    Bibliography: p.
    Includes index.
        1. Design, Industrial.   I. Title.
    TS171.L49   1988   745.2   88-7086
    ISBN 0-944327-04-4

    88 89 90 91 92   10 9 8 7 6 5 4 3 3 1

Contents

Acknowledgments

The thoughts presented in this book have taken shape over the thirty years I have spent in a product-design practice and as a result of research and the exchange of ideas with fellow designers and members of the academic community. I consider myself a chronicler or a moderator of this fascinating discussion rather than an author of any appreciable originality.

My years with the Federal Institute of Industrial Design in Warsaw, Poland (1964–1968), were especially helpful in the formation of ideas. I was most influenced by Alicja Zdybel, Bronek Sztatler, Tadeusz Pszenicki, Jerzy Slowikowski, Zbigniew Kaplan, Michel Millot (recently president of Solus Design in Paris), and, above all, by the president of the institute, Bogdan Czekaluk, who provided vision and leadership. All of them and many others contributed greatly to my understanding of the human side of the industry.

Professor Stefan Morawski of the Philosophy Department at Warsaw University was the first person outside the institute to offer advice. Through him I met Dr. Jadwiga Slawinska of Wroclaw Polytechnic, who was an inexhaustible source of ideas, enthusiasm, and encouragement.

I will always be indebted to a great architect, professor Jerzy Hryniewiecki of Warsaw Technical University, for his guidance and the time he shared with me before I left Poland in 1971.

In North America I have had the privilege of working with and learning from two leading industrial designers: Jim Shook, now Manager of Industrial Design with Tandem Computers in San Jose, California, and Morley Smith, president of Guillon, Smith, Marquart & Associates in Montreal, Canada.

I am grateful to Dr. Steve Palmer, professor in the Department of Psychology at the University of California at Berkeley, and Dr. Robert Zimbardo, professor in the Department of Psychology at Stanford University for their advice in choosing reviewers.

The reviewers greatly improved the book. They saved the text from the muddling of substance and style. My thanks go to Dr. Carlo Piccione of the Department of Psychology at Stanford University, Dr. Kathy Hemenway, formerly with AT&T Bell Telephone Laboratory, Dr. Lydia Goehr of the Department of Philosophy at the University of Nevada, Reno, Dr. Peter Pfaelzer, professor of mechanical engineering with San Francisco State University, and Dr. Robert Solso, chairman of the Department of Psychology at the University of Nevada, Reno. Their insight, recommendations, and encouragement left a lasting imprint on the book. Any inadequacies of the text remain, of course, solely my own responsibility.

My special thanks go to the proofreaders, Hugh Smith and Tom Whitehead from Western Nevada Community College. Their patience and stamina were astounding and their contribution to the book went far beyond the matters of syntax and style.

And finally, this book would not have been written if it had not been for my wife, Eva, who has been standing by me through good times and bad.

Introduction

When choosing a product we judge its functionality, sturdiness, and price, but we also judge its appearance. Sometimes the look of a product influences us in a dramatic way.

I.1 Has This Ever Happened to You?

You enter a large department store to buy a home appliance. You browse hesitantly among the multitude of products on display but nothing seems to catch your eye. You see row after row of similar appliances, and comparing prices seems to be the most interesting of your possibilities.

Suddenly you feel a thrill of excitement! What a beautiful piece of equipment! You feel an intense pleasure just looking at it and you want to buy it immediately. No, wait a minute! You try to control your emotions; you listen to the arguments of the salesperson; you think of your budget. Nothing seems to change your urge for owning the object of your sudden affection. It is as if a force beyond your control were compelling you to buy this product and no other—now!

What makes us instantly like an object? The situation described above raises an intriguing question about product development: Can this type of reaction be made to work for us when we introduce a new product into the market?

Of all the avenues available for action, attention to a product's appearance promises the manufacturer one of the highest returns on investment. Is it not true that it does not necessarily take more time and money to paint a good picture than to paint a bad one? The legendary early Ford Mustang met a broad market acceptance not because more money was spent on its development than was spent on other cars but because it embodied that mystique of a good product that expresses itself in, among other qualities, attractive appearance.

That is the topic of this book. What makes some products more attractive than others? How can the appearance of products be improved? How can a product designer use esthetic incentive to motivate a potential buyer?

Although I hope the subject of product esthetics will interest the average reader, the greatest benefits of reading this book will go to those actively engaged in product development. If you are a product designer, an inventor, a design engineer, a product development manager, or an executive, this book will help you to understand how you may increase profits safely and easily by appealing to the human search for beauty. A good-looking product always sells better than one that is equally useful but judged less attractive.

I am sure you will find it reassuring that your interest in product esthetics may be justified by much more than just expectations of material reward. People are simply happier and more fulfilled if they live in a pleasant visual environment. Consequently, a designer who pays attention to the appearance of designed products can make an important contribution to the well-being of others.

I.2 The Method

A theory of visual beauty with which everyone would agree simply does not exist. Instead, there are many explanations as to why people consider some objects attractive and not others. Are we born with esthetic preferences or do we acquire them? Is beauty "objective"—that is, does it belong to an object the same way as the object's weight or size does? Or is it "subjective," the product of a viewer's perception, different from individual to individual? Can the visual quality of the industrial product be actively pursued or is it just the result of adhering to the requirements of the product's function and manufacture?

The reality of product development for a competitive market does not easily tolerate this type of hesitation. In product design a good decision today is frequently better than an excellent one tomorrow. In a way, we repeatedly face problems similar to that of the Gordian knot. Gordius, ancient king of Phrygia, tied an enormous knot that, according to prophecy, could be undone only by the person who was to rule Asia. The knot resisted the ablest men in Greece until it was brought to the king of Macedonia, Alexander the Great. He solved the problem with one blow of his sword; he cut the knot in two. In a way, Alexander applied an engineering solution to the problem.

The approach to issues of esthetics in this book can be compared with that of an engineer solving problems not yet fully analyzed by science. Shigley and Mitchel (1983, 274) write: "Engineers use science to solve their problems *if* the science is available. But available or not, the problem must be solved, and whatever form the solution takes under those conditions is called engineering."

An example of another engineering solution is found in the classic story, "The Columbus Egg." It is said that in the time of Columbus a game was played in the taverns of Genoa at the expense of local fools. They were asked to set an egg on the table upright and on its narrower end. There was a lot of laughter at the sight of a poor fellow hopelessly trying to perform the task. Columbus managed it nonetheless. He struck the table with an egg, breaking its shell at the narrow end far enough to immobilize the egg in an upright position. Thus, he applied an engineering solution to a seemingly unsolvable problem.

The usefulness of many practical solutions is the result of their simplicity and directness rather than a mere following of elaborate rules. As we will see in the course of this book, it is the urgency of practical situations that will sometimes lead us to shortcuts and simplifications that might be questioned in a purely theoretical proposition.

This book will not introduce new facts. However, using available bodies of information, we will try to achieve a new balance or relative harmony among them for the purpose of design.

3

This book is purposely eclectic; we will draw on the findings of various disciplines. The process of design will be the unifying element and the focus for all the available components. Their usefulness will be assessed with respect to the design process.

I.3 The Idea

Life can be seen as a continual adaptation of humans to biological and social changes. There are two types of human adaptational activities. One type is *automatic*, the other is *rational*.

Some automatic responses are *inborn*. The retina of our eye automatically narrows when exposed to excessive light; without a conscious effort on our part, the heartbeat increases when more oxygen is needed in the blood.

Other automatic responses are *learned*. A boxer automatically avoids the punches of his opponent without thinking about it. He has learned the correct technique beforehand in the gym. Our knowledge that dirt is the home of bacteria and the source of a foul taste makes us automatically reject a dirty spoon in disgust.

Rational responses are different. When solving a scientific problem, choosing a stock for investment, or buying a house, we devote time to the project; we read, argue, and compare until we are ready to make a decision.

In real life, the two types of response—automatic and rational—are usually combined. In addition, feelings and emotions accompany all our activities, the automatic as well as those resulting from reasoning. However, the presence of emotion is more prominent in our automatic reactions to life changes. This is why we refer to some of these types of reaction as "emotional." We sometimes say, "Don't be emotional", meaning: "Don't jump to conclusions. Think, take your time, be rational."

We pride ourselves on being rational beings. Educators try to teach people to be rational, but emotions nonetheless play a fundamental role in determining our behavior. We will examine evidence that emotions seem to express the memory of our past experiences. In effect, emotions provide information about the value for us of the situations that initiate them. Positive emotions prompt us to accept a situation, and negative emotions cause us to act defensively. Emotions have a utilitarian value.

It may be argued that our emotional reactions are of poorer quality than the rational ones. However, their great value lies in the speed with which they occur. That speed of reaction is very important. Emotions control the first line of defense in many life situations and they effectively guide us toward potential rewards.

In this book we will treat esthetic emotion as one of the family of emotions that humans experience—the one generated by the appearance of objects. Within this framework the primary function of esthetic emotions, a justification for their existence, is similar to that of other emotions. We will present evidence that esthetic emotions also warn us about surrounding objects and situations or testify to their apparent suitability for us. We will see that, like other emotions, esthetic emotions are rather poor indicators of the real value of an object to us. The utility of esthetic emotions lies in the speed with which they convey information.

Esthetic emotions related to our *inborn* involuntary behavior indicate to what degree the visual environment is acceptable to our sense of sight. The understanding of this process is still in the preliminary stages. The Gestalt school of psychology has been one of the branches of science investigating the subject. Cybernetics and computer science today provide powerful analogies for the way the brain analyzes what the eye sees. Very slowly, an understanding has emerged that there is an inborn need for some measure of organization, regularity, or simplicity in visual patterns in order that they can be observed and analyzed by the brain with a degree of comfort. The occurrence of such a degree of visual comfort when we observe visual patterns disposes us agreeably toward them, while chaos in the field of vision generates emotions of impatience and rejection.

At this level of concern for esthetic emotions, only a narrow and vague border separates them from those factors that are of interest to human engineering. Human engineering, sometimes called ergonomics, is a discipline concerned with the acceptable limits for the human environment of perception, light intensity, temperature, noise, available space, and so on. For the purpose of this book it will be enough to indicate that the difference lies in the way each discipline approaches the process of seeing. Human engineering is interested in quantity, measurement, and time of response; esthetics is concerned with value, judgment, and generated emotion.

Esthetic emotions related to *learned* involuntary behavior also have the primary function of warning us or of disposing us agreeably toward the objects perceived. In this case, however, the feeling of pleasure or discomfort in the presence of the observed object is not derived from inborn reactions but must have been conditioned in the past. The role of past experience is indispensable in the generation of this type of esthetic emotion.

It is quite possible that because of past mental associations that have developed between various life situations and their accompanying visual patterns that, for example, garden furniture in white, orange, or blue will be found attractive and will sell better than that in black, gray, or brown. Similarly, a person raised in the city welcomes, on his return from the countryside, the granite and glass blocks of Manhattan, whereas a farmer from Idaho in the same situation would be repelled by the oily waters of the Hudson River and the lack of an open horizon.

I have examined the subject long enough to bet any amount of money that at this particular moment there must be at least one reader who will protest vehemently: "Baloney! I like black garden furniture!" And there will be another one arguing: "But my uncle from Idaho just loves New York!"

This is quite understandable. People differ widely in their inborn capacities for emotional response, even more so with responses conditioned by experience. It is doubtful that a law of esthetics that would be equivalent to Newton's law of gravity will ever be formulated. Esthetics is a different field of knowledge. Will mathematics ever find here an application?

Perhaps the thought of journalist Alfred Runyon that "the race is not always to the swift nor the battle to the strong—but that's the way to bet" applies as well to esthetic preferences. Can we not safely say that light, sunny colors are not always preferred in garden furniture, but this is the way to bet?

Design usually responds to the emergence of some need. It may be said that designers aim at fulfilling a particular need, and this is why the concept of need will play an important role in our bringing together the available pieces of information. I believe that nature has not developed any human capacity that, in its conception, would not serve human interest. Some need, rational or not, underlies all human behavior. Accordingly, the question of why some industrial products are considered more attractive then others of the same class will be approached with human needs in mind.

One of the researchers of human needs was psychologist Abraham Maslow. He showed all human needs as forming a spectrum, similar to the band of colors produced when sunlight is passed through a prism. This spectrum reaches from such basic bodily needs as hunger to such complex psychological needs as, for instance, the need for prestige.

Maslow's research will serve us well. His concept of a spectrum of needs describes the complexity but also the unity of human nature in one powerful symbol. In addition, the reference to Maslow may increase the accessibility of the text. Many engineers and designers have surely been exposed to his gradation of needs while studying motivation during management courses.

And finally, Maslow's spectrum of needs will help us to reconcile to some degree the difficulties of esthetics. One of the hotly debated issues is, for instance, whether esthetic preferences are inborn or acquired. However, when analyzed with human needs in mind, the two approaches begin to lose their antagonistic edge. Both become accepted, each more suited to one of the two ends of the spectrum of needs.

Our esthetic tastes and preferences may be mysterious and often seemingly absurd, but there is no reason to consider them unexplained. In the words of Polonius when speaking of Hamlet's conduct: "Though this be madness, yet there is method in't" (Shakespeare, *Hamlet*, act 1, scene 2).

When describing the origins of esthetic emotions, I always purposely emphasize the utilitarian values lying at their roots. However, the unusual human capacity for play, experimentation, and creation does something surprising to esthetic experience: it raises esthetic emotions to the level of autonomy. Esthetic emotions become something that we actively look for, that we expect from life. It is as if our capacity for esthetic appreciation were seeking liberation from the service to which it has been called, reaching for an independence from purpose, seeking pure enjoyment. We start to enjoy esthetic emotions for themselves alone, with total indifference to, or lack of awareness of, their origins and purpose. The pursuit of beauty becomes the goal itself.

This separation from any evident purpose, this manifest impracticality is, of course, the fundamental characteristic of esthetic preference. However, it is only natural that while investigating the esthetic values of industrial products rather than those of works of art, we will maintain a high awareness of the linkage of purpose that exists between esthetic emotions and the utilitarian values that were present at their origins.

I support the traditional interpretation of esthetic value; that is, only sight and sound are commonly accepted esthetic stimuli. Touch, taste, and smell values in esthetic experience have been at best vague and ambiguous, and they have not yet been the subject of serious examination.

In addition, an esthetic analysis of sound is traditionally limited to the analysis of music or language. The scope of this book does not, of course, include sound.

Consequently, the esthetic value of, let us say, an automobile will be determined only by the level of the positive emotions generated by its appearance. The softness and smell of its upholstery, the comfort of its seats, the responsiveness of its suspension, the sounds generated by the automobile, and so on, remain outside the scope of the book.

It is true that our final evaluation of an industrial product—what we feel and think about it—is the result of a complex process that includes senses other than seeing and includes "thinking with words" about the utility of the product as well. However, this book is not about the complex and all-embracing process of evaluation. Instead, it is concerned solely with the very special value of an industrial product that is responsible for our animation at the mere sight of that product. Therefore, in this book, only this animation is identified with esthetic emotion. Such an approach is in agreement with the tradition whereby seeing has always remained the central fascination of esthetics; and such an interpretation coincides with the popular understanding of the terms of esthetic value and esthetic emotion. Beauty lies in the *eye* of the beholder and not in the nose of one who smells or the skin of one who touches.

I.4 The Presentation

I have tried to make this book as accessible as possible. In appreciation of the reader's time, the book is purposely concise. Its information is arranged in sections of growing complexity. You can spend as much time with the book as you wish and you can learn as much as you want to learn.

It is possible, for instance, that at first you will read no more than this introduction. Later you may read part 1, which is a self-contained unit telling the complete story in the simplest way by using illustrations as a primary means of communication. The illustrations are supported with concise modules of text.

Part 2—the principal text of the book—develops and reinforces the main ideas outlined in part 1. Not all of the illustrations are referred to in the text and not all parts of the text have their equivalent in the illustrations. Nevertheless, there is a clear parallel between the two sections. Even though both have been designed to stand alone, they supplement each other and to some degree show the same problems from slightly different angles.

Chapter 1 of part 2 reviews the concepts of human needs, form, beauty, expression, esthetic value and esthetic emotion. This represents cleaning the workplace, so to speak, before starting the real work. The concept of *needs* is essential to the book; one of its premises is that esthetic preferences reflect our sensitivity to the needs encountered in life in a very perverse way—not obvious but hidden to our power of analysis. There is always confusion in the understanding of the terms *form, beauty, expression, esthetic value* and *esthetic emotion* as they are applied to the development of attractive industrial products. Therefore, defining these terms as they are used in the book seems appropriate.

To develop the idea of esthetic preferences being a complex function of needs, chapter 2 presents to the reader how humans, as self-regulating systems, work in their changing biological, social, economic, and cultural environments. Automatic patterns of behavior are given special attention because they lead to further investigation. First, a broad panorama of human behavior is rendered and then, by narrowing the field of attention, esthetic preferences are presented in the context of human adaptational activities.

For the purpose of methodology, chapter 3 divides the esthetic values of industrial products into three groups: X—derived from visual order, Y—related to functionality, and Z—conducive to the visual culture of the time. Finally, all the previous discussions lead to the pivotal section of the book, 3.10, which outlines esthetic mediation in a product-design process. The summary recapitulates the major points of the book.

The commentaries and bibliography (part 3) provide references to the literature on the subject, more pertinent facts, and a helpful guide for further study.

The commentaries replace traditional footnotes. Considering the mental concentration required to follow a relatively exotic subject, it has occurred to me that footnotes might cause some distraction to the average reader. Consequently, footnotes have been eliminated from the main text. Instead, a special section of the book (part 3) has been added to accommodate those readers with the highest interest in the subject, those with more stamina or with a greater desire to get ahead.

The commentaries have grown in a way which I can only describe as natural. I wrote each of them only when I thought that additional information could lead to a better understanding of a given topic. Accordingly, some sections of particular chapters do not have any associated commentaries, while others have many. Some commentaries are just one- or two-line notes; others are short essays on selected subjects. Here are examples of topics investigated in the commentaries:

— Why can product esthetics be pursued as a separate subject?
— Can "industrial design" be successfully defined as a discipline?
— What is a *golden mean*?
— If functionality leads to an attractive form, why are some functional products ugly?

You may not read the commentaries at all and still learn the most useful information on the subject. You may read appropriate parts of the commentaries after each chapter or chapter section. You may read them separately, all together, or in parts. The number of possibilities for increasing your enjoyment of reading and learning is almost unlimited, and the choice is yours.

In essence, the book is written in such a way that its three parts represent increasing complexity and a gradually increasing challenge to the reader.

There is another transition occurring in the book as the text unfolds: the gradual transition from certainty to controversy and ambiguity. Part 1 is constructed as though it presented an unchallenged truth—objective knowledge solidly resting on the body of the available facts. Such a construction has been dictated by the needs and expectations of the average, projected reader of this book. The average reader is not interested in theoretical controversies and will, in the first place, look for advice presented in a measured and tidy way. In fact, however, any sort of apparent order cannot reflect the reality of the issues of esthetics. At best it reflects the thrust of this book as described in its subtitle, that is just an *interpretation*, a personal view of things. In contrast to part 1, the subsequent parts of the book provide some insight into the nature of the controversies of esthetics.

Nearing the close of the introduction, let me recapitulate my expectations regarding this book. In short, the intention of the book is to clarify the mystery of esthetic preferences and to sharpen your competitive edge in the field of product development. Designers whose intuitive responses to design problems have been formed by, among other factors, the knowledge of the theory of esthetic value, remarkably increase their chances of designing a product of broad market acceptance. This was probably what the great architect Walter Gropius had in mind when he advised designers to first acquire knowledge and then let themselves be led by inspiration.

Part 1

1

Let's Start It the Easy Way: Illustrations

Life can be defined as a chain of events whose purpose is to maintain the balance between people and the world around them.

Every time the balance is disturbed, someone experiences a need.

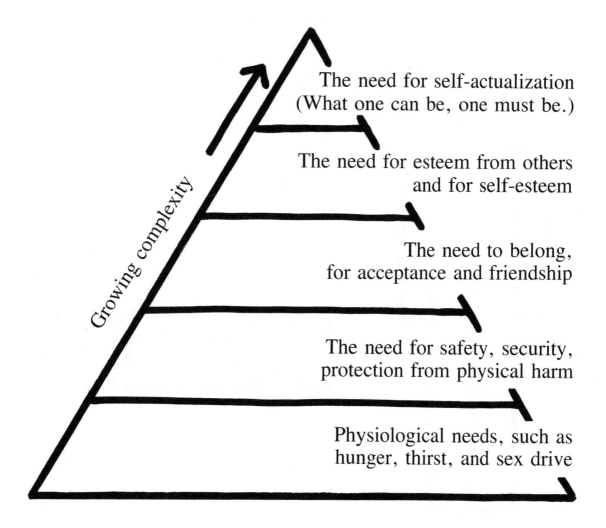

The need for self-actualization
(What one can be, one must be.)

The need for esteem from others
and for self-esteem

The need to belong,
for acceptance and friendship

The need for safety, security,
protection from physical harm

Physiological needs, such as
hunger, thirst, and sex drive

Growing complexity

The pyramid above arranges human needs from basic cravings to complex desires for personal growth and fulfillment.

Figure 1

To investigate the role of the esthetic values of industrial products in satisfying human needs, we will adopt the language of cybernetics.

In this language, life organisms are biological systems. Machines, apparatus, and instruments are technical systems.

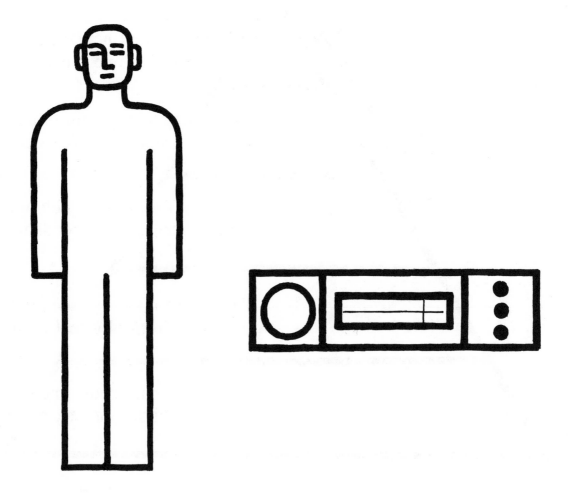

The human is
a biological system

A radio is
a technical system.

Figure 2

16

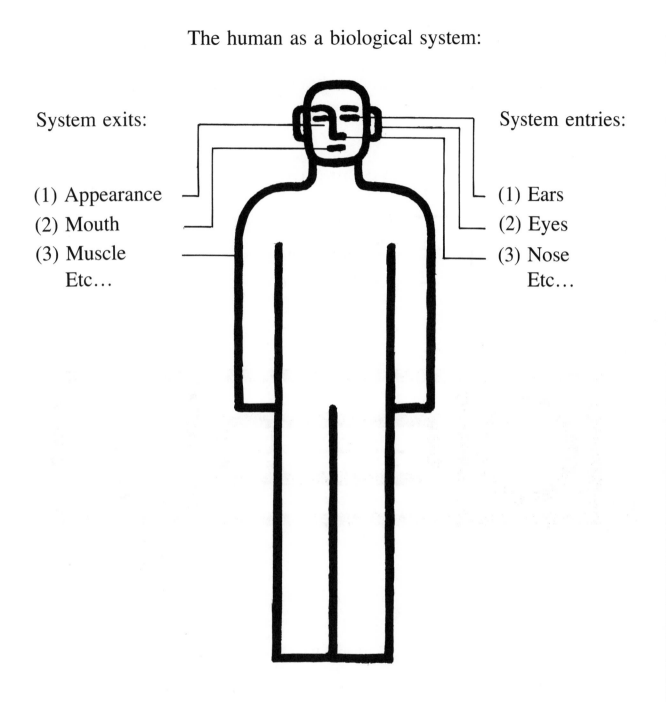

The human as a biological system:

System exits:

(1) Appearance
(2) Mouth
(3) Muscle
    Etc...

System entries:

(1) Ears
(2) Eyes
(3) Nose
    Etc...

Systems affect the world around them or receive stimuli from it through the specific gates referred to as external exits and entries.

Figure 3

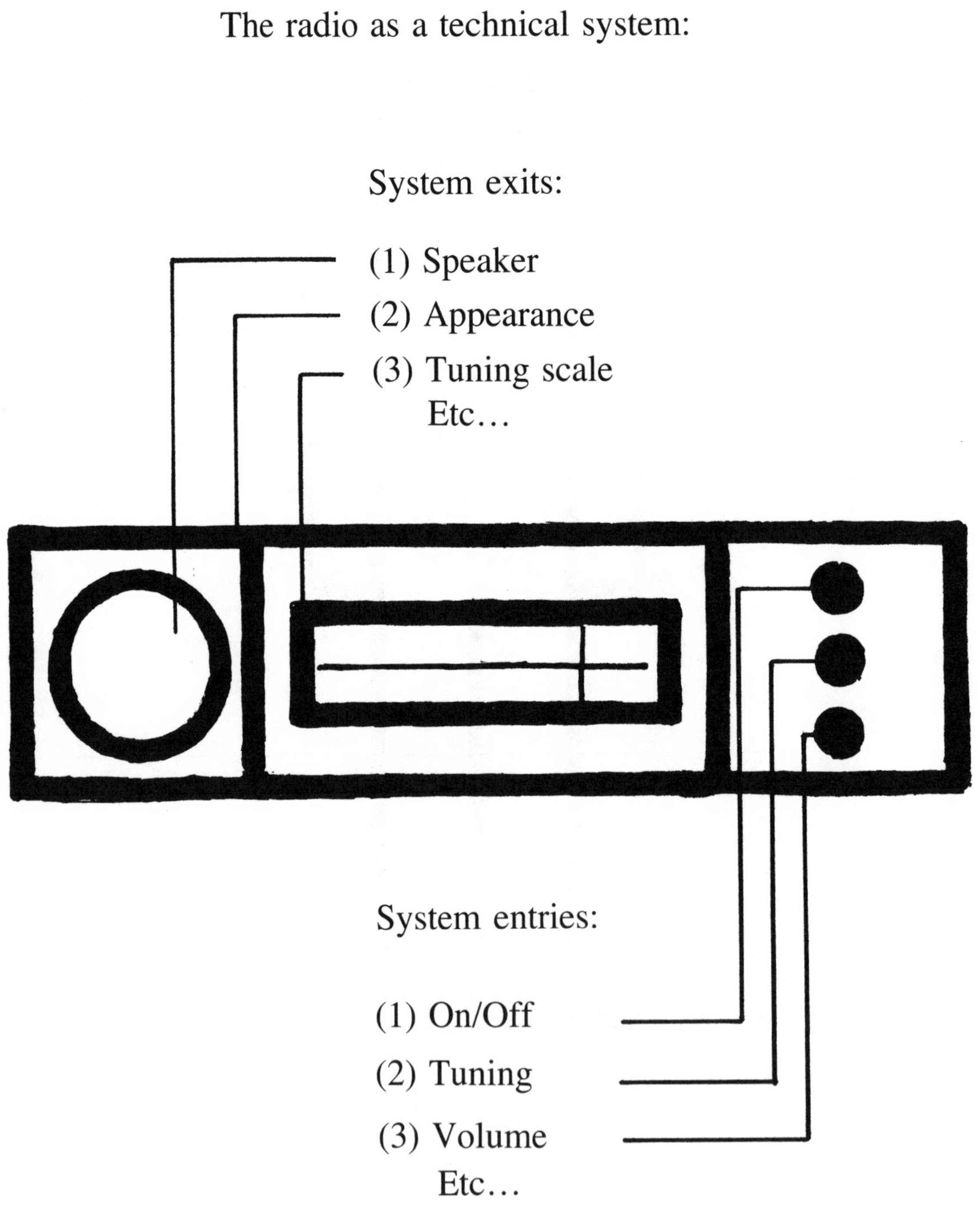

The radio as a technical system:

System exits:

(1) Speaker

(2) Appearance

(3) Tuning scale
Etc…

System entries:

(1) On/Off

(2) Tuning

(3) Volume
Etc…

Figure 4

The sum of all the external entries and exits of the system makes its form.

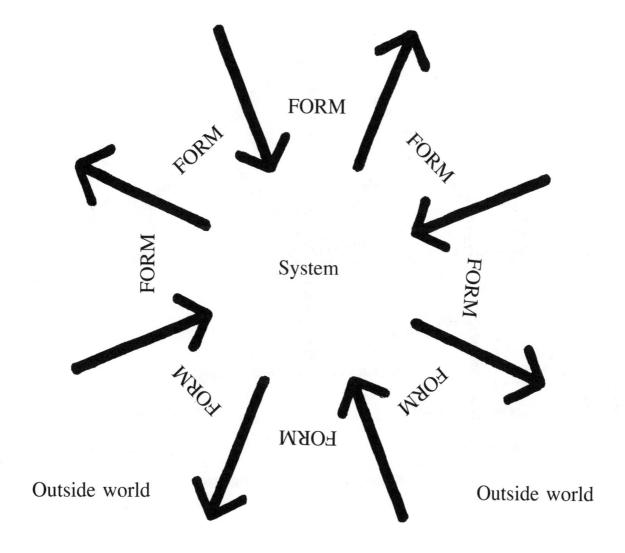

Form is the only means through which the system can engage in relationships with the outside world.

Figure 5

19

A mechanism of balancing the processes inside any system and between systems is that of feedback. See how this mechanism works by analyzing the action of Watt's governor controlling the revolutions of the steam engine.

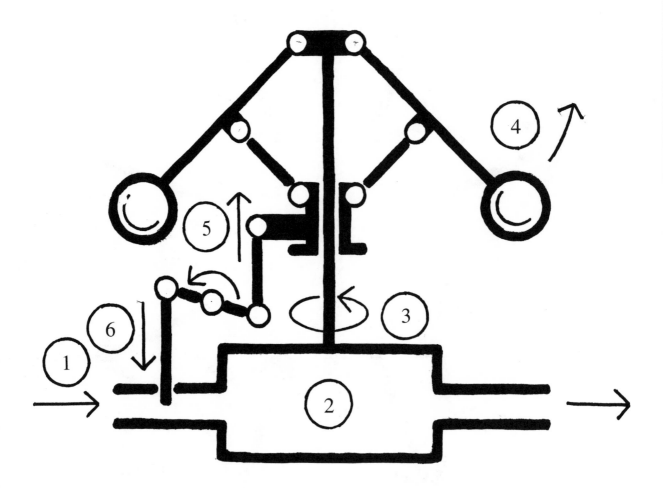

(1) Increased pressure of steam
(2) brings the engine up
(3) to higher rpm's
(4) which cause the governor weights to fly away from the shaft.
(5) The action of weights makes the lever move,
(6) close the throttle, and reduce rpm's.

Figure 6

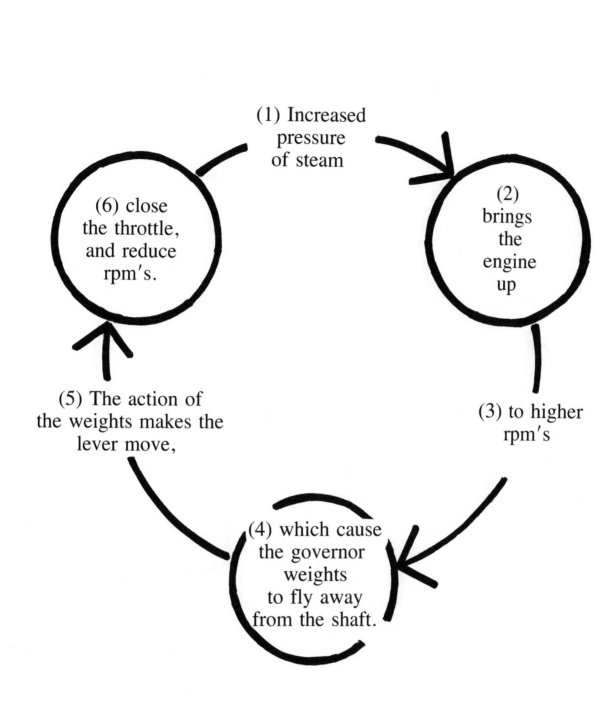

Diagram of Watt's governor feedback mechanism.

Figure 7

21

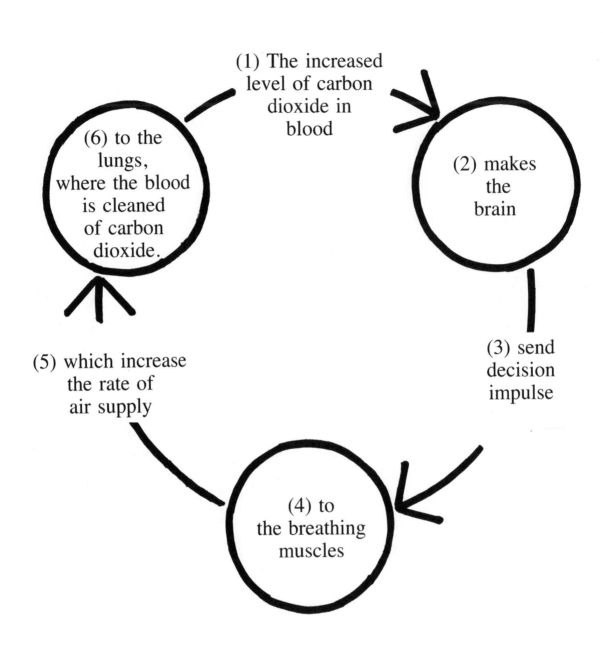

(1) The increased level of carbon dioxide in blood

(2) makes the brain

(3) send decision impulse

(4) to the breathing muscles

(5) which increase the rate of air supply

(6) to the lungs, where the blood is cleaned of carbon dioxide.

The principle is the same for biological systems...

Figure 8

...and for the feedback between biological and technical systems.

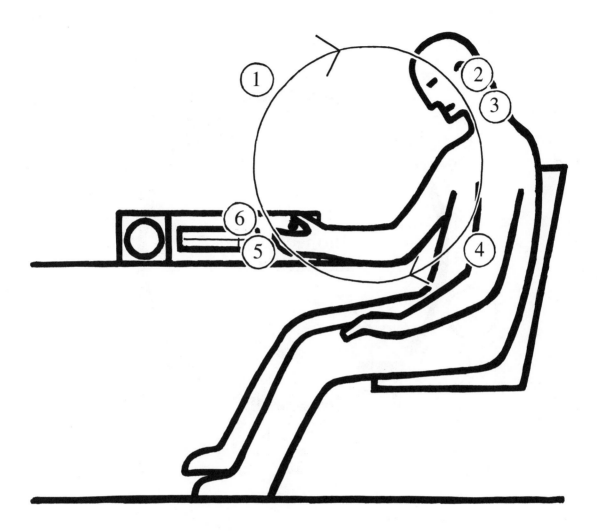

(1) The annoying sound of the radio
(2) makes the brain
(3) send a decision impulse
(4) to the muscles of the hand
(5) which change the position of the volume adjuster
(6) and reduces the level of sound.

Figure 9

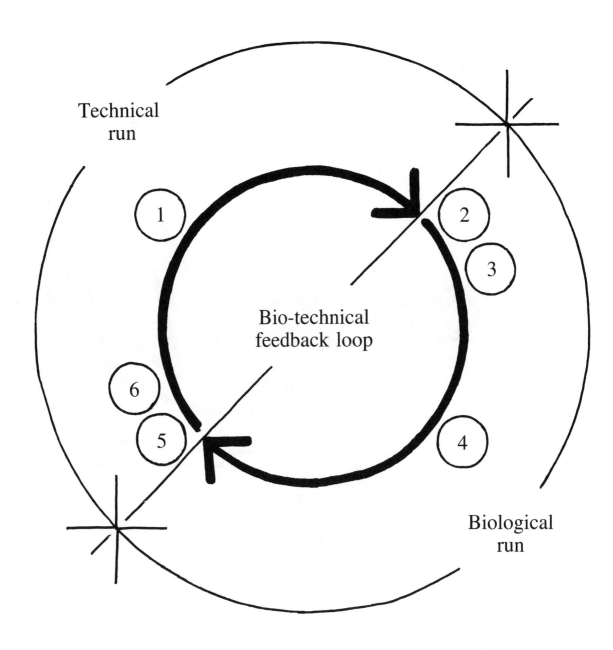

The feedback loop shown in figure 9 consists of two halves: one runs through the technical system, the other one through the biological system.

Figure 10

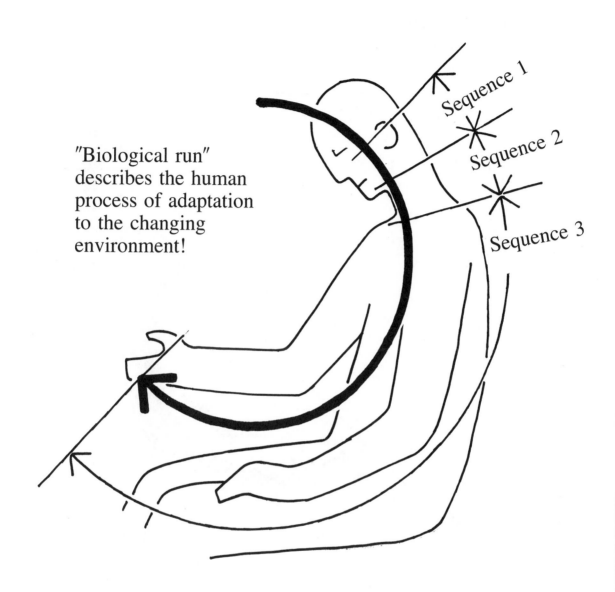

"Biological run" describes the human process of adaptation to the changing environment!

Three sequences will always occur in the "biological run" of every bio-technical feedback loop:

Sequence 1: **Input**—reception of information
Sequence 2: **Analysis** of information and decision making
Sequence 3: **Output**—response

Figure 11

25

At the end of analysis, an emotion emerges. Emotion directs and motivates response.

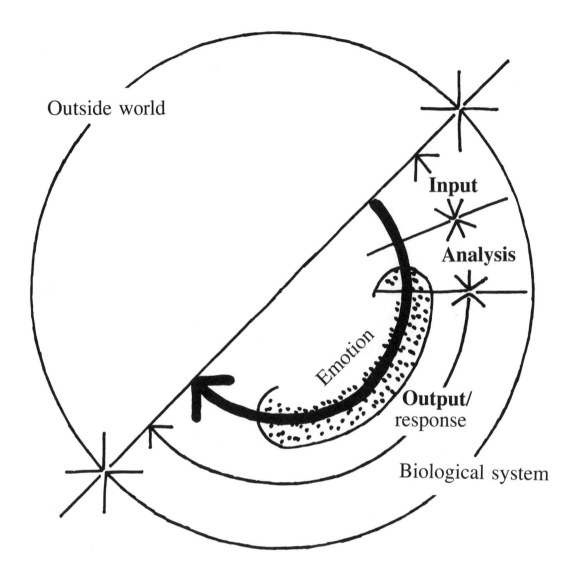

Emotion is an indicator of the apparent value of the stimulus received from the outside world.

Positive emotion generates an assimilative response. Negative emotion generates a rejection.

Figure 12

Examples below, reading from the bottom up, show that human adaptational processes vary from simple to very complex.

CASE (F) A scientific experiment engages the highest level of abstract thinking.

(E) A stalled engine challenges the motorist's know-how.

(D) A blunt tool will be rejected after a couple of turns.

(C) The cry of the animal mobilizes the hunter.

(B) A burned hand is quickly retracted.

(A) A drop in atmospheric pressure results in accelerated breathing.

Growing complexity →

In the majority of cases (A, B, C, D) the processes of analysis and decision making are automatic, with emotion as the only motivator.

In complex processes (cases E and F), emotion shares its motivational function with rational thinking.

Figure 13

27

Each of the adaptational processes described in figure 13 has three sequences.

The type of process	1. **Input**	2. **Analysis**	3. **Output**
(F) Conducting a scientific experiment	A sequence of visual stimuli	Rational	Test report
(E) Starting a stalled engine	—"—	—"—	Ignition of engine
(D) Forming matter	The sight of a poorly machined part	Reflexive	Rejection of the part
(C) Hunting	The cry of an animal	—"—	Concentration of attention
(B) Avoiding injury	Pain	—"—	Retraction of hand
(A) Controlling the supply of oxygen	Low atmospheric pressure	—"—	Accelerated breathing

Figure 14

Summary of the sequences of adaptational processes

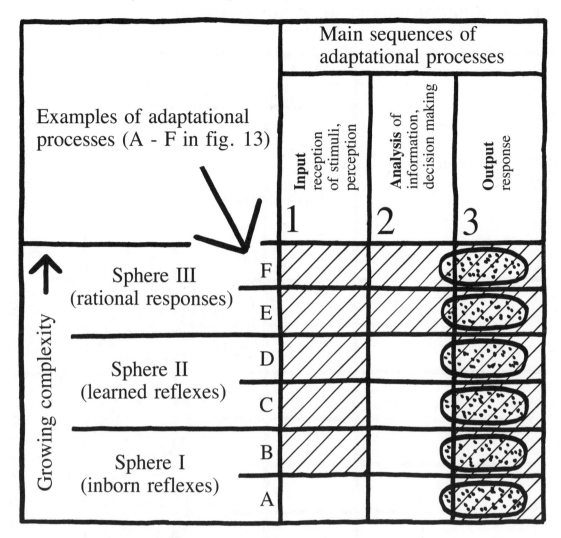

	Main sequences of adaptational processes		
Examples of adaptational processes (A - F in fig. 13)	**Input** reception of stimuli, perception 1	**Analysis of** information, decision making 2	**Output** response 3
Sphere III (rational responses) — F	▨	▨	⬭
Sphere III (rational responses) — E	▨	▨	⬭
Sphere II (learned reflexes) — D	▨		⬭
Sphere II (learned reflexes) — C	▨		⬭
Sphere I (inborn reflexes) — B	▨		⬭
Sphere I (inborn reflexes) — A			⬭

Growing complexity ↑

Not all of the sequences are registered by the consciousness!

▨ Registered by consciousness

☐ Outside of consciousness

⬭ Field of emotions

Figure 15

Flow of information in adaptational processes

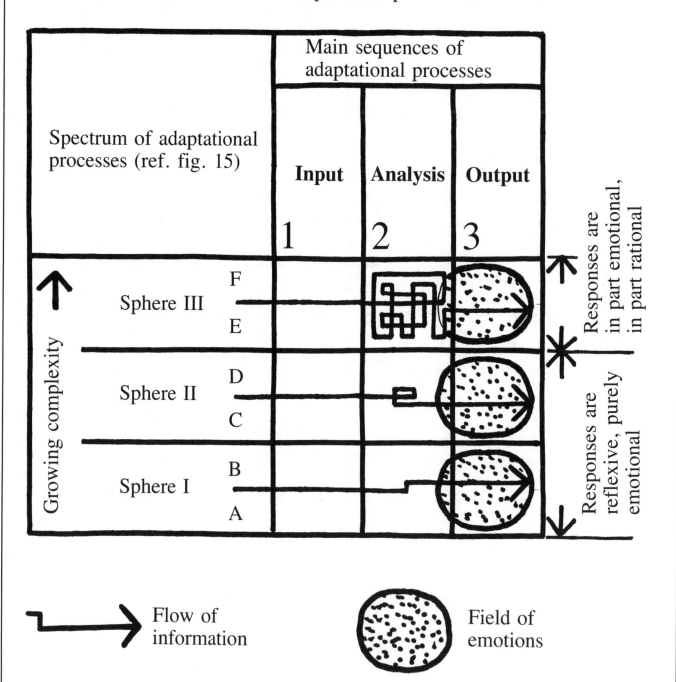

Flow of information

Field of emotions

The longer the flow of information, the longer the time of analysis.

Figure 16

Most human adaptational responses to changing environment are automatic.

In an automatic response, the time of analysis is very short because the pattern of response is either inborn or acquired and stored in the memory.

An example of automatic responses taking place in the human system is reflex. Reflexes also can be inborn or acquired (conditioned). The classical experiment illustrating the process of acquiring a reflex runs as follows:

During consumption of food the dog salivates. If just before serving the food a bell is rung, after a number of such associations between the food and the bell the dog salivates at the mere sound of the bell. Salivation has become a conditioned reflex to the stimulus of sound.

A similar pattern occurs in conditioning human automatic responses.

Figure 17

31

A driver, for instance, has to pay attention to surrounding traffic, the speedometer, stoplights, the sound of the engine, and so on. Drivers would not be able to handle all these tasks if automatic responses had not been conditioned into them in driving school or elsewhere.

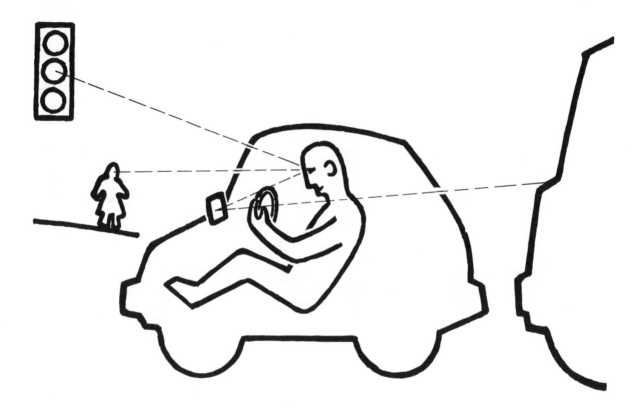

The chain of automatic responses during driving is accompanied by a stream of stronger or weaker emotions of alertness, boredom, anger, pleasure of going for a ride, and so on.

Figure 18

Rewards and punishments make the process of acquiring automatic responses more effective.

Stimulus	Reward/ punishment	Reflex
 Green light	Reward: You can now drive	The foot on the gas
 Red light	Punishment: If you drive a ticket or accident may follow	The foot on the brake
No obstacle 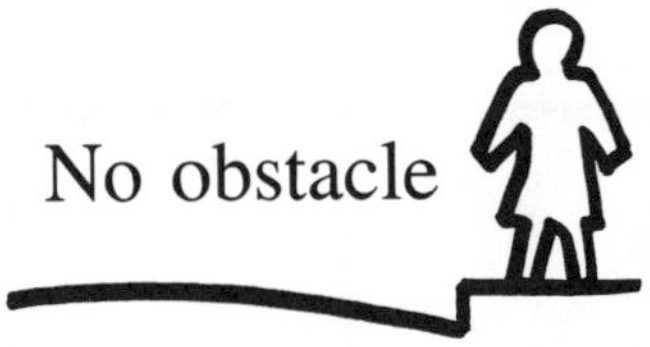	Reward: You can continue driving	The foot on the gas
 Obstacle!	Punishment: If you hit the pedestrian, an arrest or fine is imminent	The foot on the brake

Rewards are associated with positive emotions, punishments with negative ones.

Figure 19

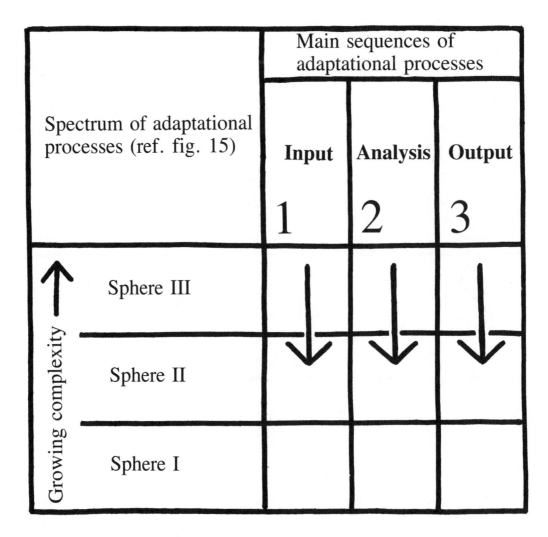

A demand for the efficiency of life processes necessitates the transformation of more complex forms of behavior into simpler ones, analytical thinking into reflexes.

Figure 20

Conscious processes of adaptation that are described by the pattern

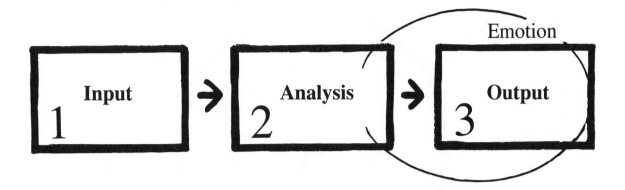

are replaced by simplified, involuntary processes.

Duration of analysis is shortened to an instant:

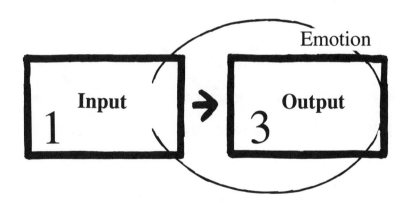

Automatic responses displace thinking; emotions displace a rational judgment.

There is a continual process of enriching the fund of our intuitive, emotional responses to the world around us.

Figure 21

35

Some emotions are esthetic emotions.

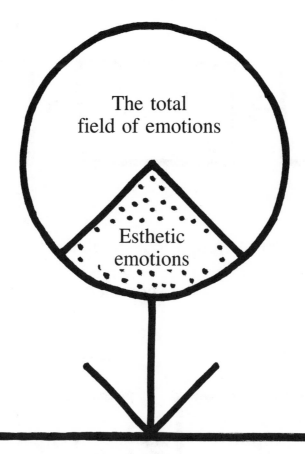

The total
field of emotions

Esthetic
emotions

(1) are generated by visual stimuli, the appearance of the object

(2) are detached from any direct practical value of the object for the viewer and

(3) develop instantaneously below the level of consciousness.

Figure 22

As with any other emotion, esthetic emotion is an indicator of the apparent value of the stimulus to the viewer.

While looking at any object, including this interceptor F-20, there will always be some explanation that is related to our unconscious needs and that either makes the object appear attractive to us or does not.

Figure 23

37

Esthetic emotion is commonplace. We experience it not only in a museum of the arts or in an opera house.

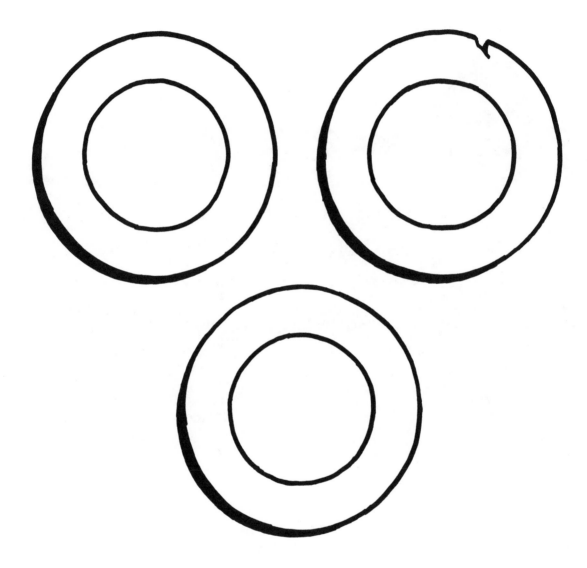

It is also an esthetic emotion that determines that the last plate to be picked up in a cafeteria will be the one, otherwise perfect, that has a small crack at the edge.

Figure 24

Since esthetic emotions are spontaneous and develop beneath the level of consciousness, their location on the diagram of adaptational processes (ref. fig. 15) will be as shown below:

Spectrum of adaptational processes (ref. fig. 15)	Main sequences of adaptational processes		
	Input 1	**Analysis** 2	**Output** 3
Sphere III			
Sphere II			Field of esthetic emotions
Sphere I			

Figure 25

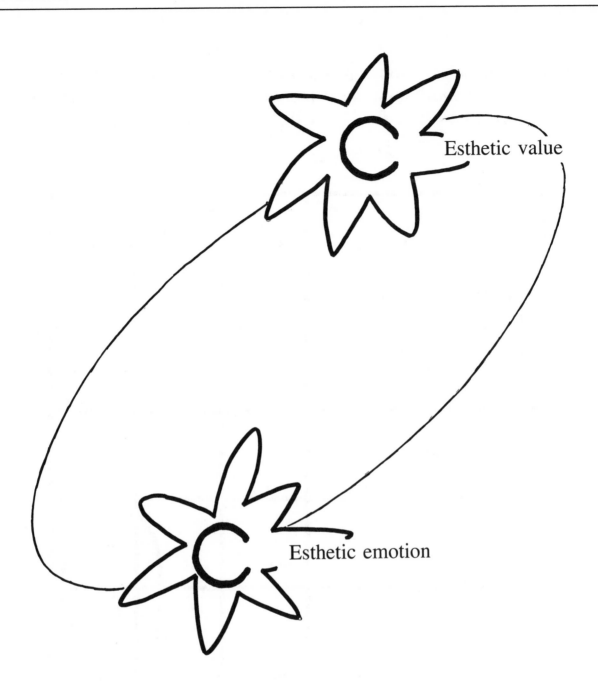

Esthetic value

Esthetic emotion

Esthetic value and esthetic emotion are terms as inseparable as twin stars: esthetic values are those values of the form that generate esthetic emotions.

Figure 26

Esthetic values of industrial products can be grouped in three blocks, starting, at the base, with those of low complexity and universal appeal, which are better suited for generalizations, to those of growing complexity, increasing subjectivity, and diminishing responsiveness to analysis.

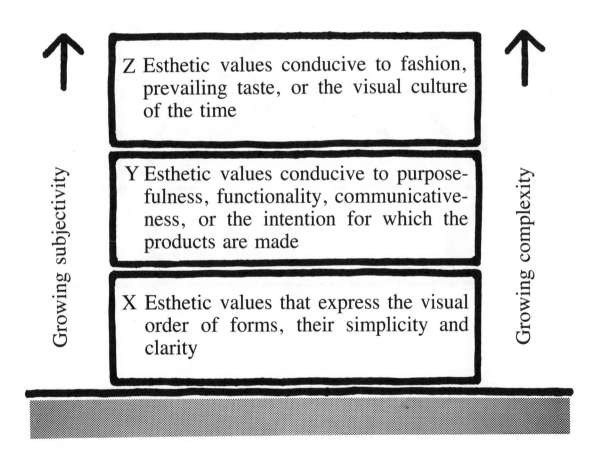

Figure 27

A "petal" diagram illustrates the overlapping of esthetic sensibilities of different generations.

The field of esthetic sensibility of…

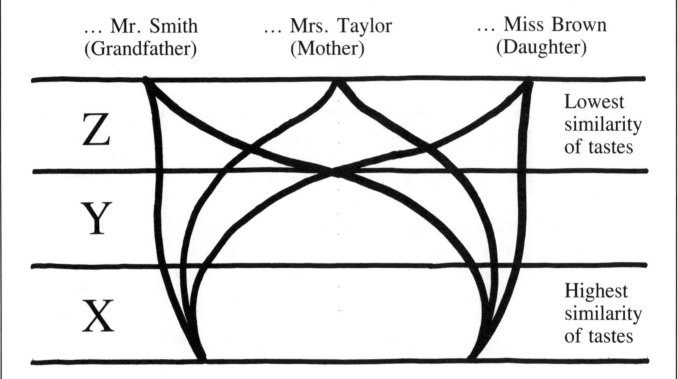

… Mr. Smith
(Grandfather)

… Mrs. Taylor
(Mother)

… Miss Brown
(Daughter)

Z

Y

X

Lowest
similarity
of tastes

Highest
similarity
of tastes

The highest similarity of esthetic preferences will be found in the sphere of X, the lowest in Z.

Figure 28

The esthetic value of visual order X is convincingly demonstrated in experiments of Gestalt psychology.

In one experiment, several people were briefly shown the following pattern:

then asked to reproduce it from memory

Results	Tendencies displayed
	Symmetry enhanced
	Overall shape simplified
	Closing of boundaries
	Repetition of similar shape

Conclusion: If, in design, we follow these tendencies, we will invite favorable reception.

Figure 29

What is wrong with the figures on the left?

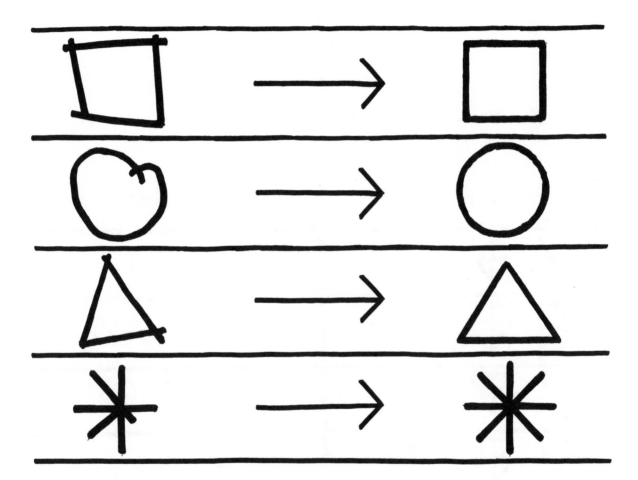

Corrections were asked for, which led consistently to the restoration of regularity and simplicity.

Figure 30

Simpler does not necessarily mean consisting of a smaller number of elements. The square will commonly be considered to be simpler than the triangle even though the square is composed of a greater number of components.

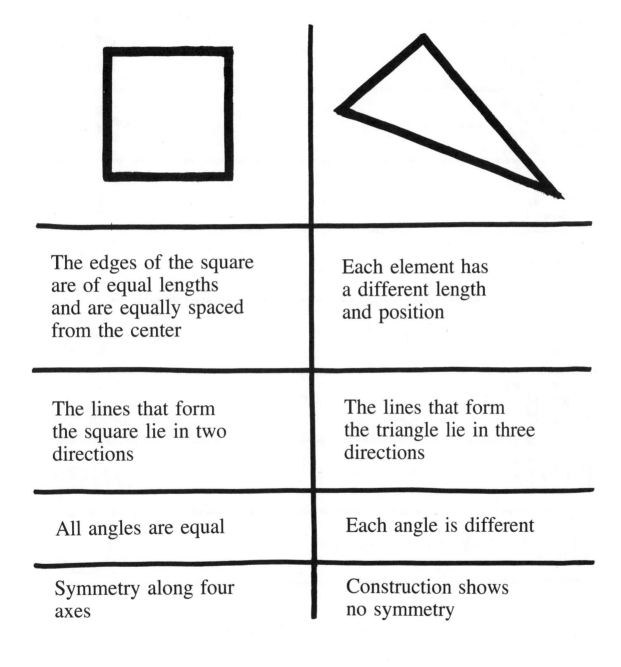

The edges of the square are of equal lengths and are equally spaced from the center	Each element has a different length and position
The lines that form the square lie in two directions	The lines that form the triangle lie in three directions
All angles are equal	Each angle is different
Symmetry along four axes	Construction shows no symmetry

Figure 31

Gestalt psychology identifies several characteristics of visual patterns that aid perception of forms.

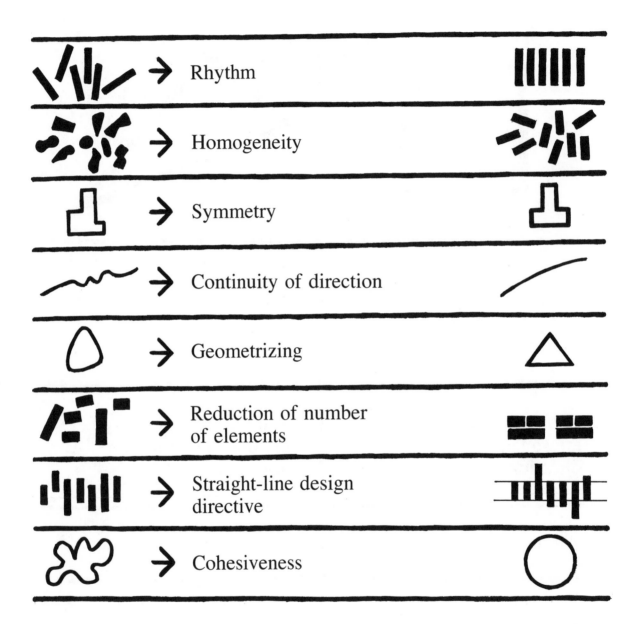

Rhythm

Homogeneity

Symmetry

Continuity of direction

Geometrizing

Reduction of number of elements

Straight-line design directive

Cohesiveness

Let us now examine the listed characteristics one by one.

Figure 32

Rhythm is the repetition of visual elements related by similarity of shape, position in space, color, and so on.

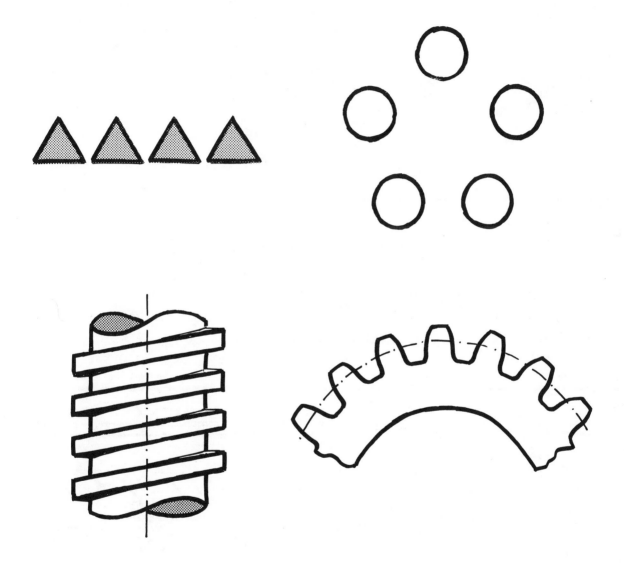

Besides the rigid, mechanical rhythms such as those of a gear or threaded bolt, there exist...

Figure 33

47

…subtle and lively rhythms typical of nature. Pebbles on the beach and the waves behind them provide a sense of rhythm. Flowers in a meadow, despite differences in shape and size, make up a field of unquestionably rhythmic character. This type of loose rhythm makes a foundation of visual homogeneity.

Figure 34

Homogeneity, closely related to rhythm, is the standardization of the means of expression.

The square is more homogeneous than the contrasting figure. Its homogeneity comes out of the standardization of straight sections making up its edges and angles. The resulting angles are also standardized.

Figure 35

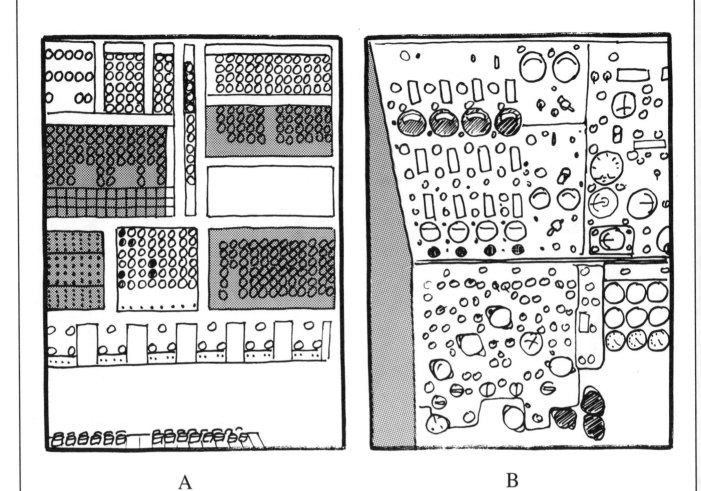

A　　　　　　　　　　　　B

The higher visual unity and organization of the board *A* as compared with a makeshift test board *B* is the result of its homogeneity. Only two types of shapes have been used in its design: a circle and a rectangle.

Board *A* will also usually be preferred since it has a smaller numbr of more easily perceived blocks as opposed to the multitude of elements competing for attention in board *B*.

Figure 36

The appearance of a lathe was improved through the application of the principle of homogeneity. The concept of similar rectangle was applied in shaping the major elements of its form. The shapes of its controls are now more closely related.

Figure 37

Symmetry is a condition where one half of the pattern is the mirror image of the other half. The number of axes of symmetry for various shapes:

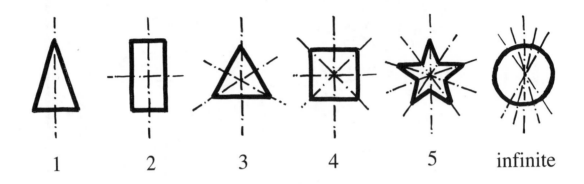

| 1 | 2 | 3 | 4 | 5 | infinite |

Symmetrical patterns attract because of their greater organization.

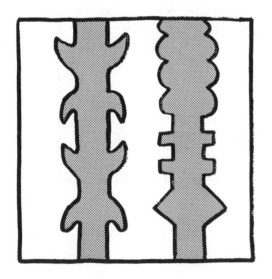 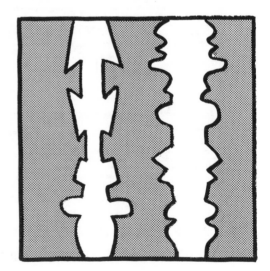

Figure 38

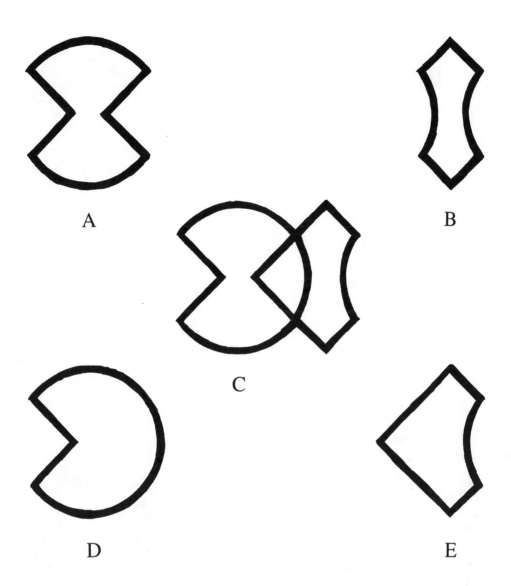

Continuity of direction has a stronger appeal than symmetry. Two symmetrical figures, *A* and *B*, having been brought together, assume the different identities of figures *D* and *E*. The new patterns have lost their original symmetry. However, they display a greater continuity of contour lines.

Figure 39

53

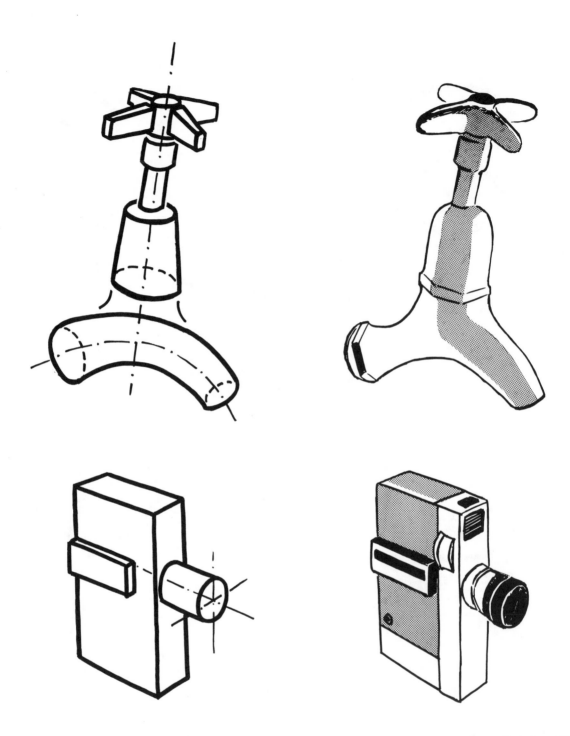

Geometrizing of visual patterns has an exceptional value for facilitation of perception.

Figure 40

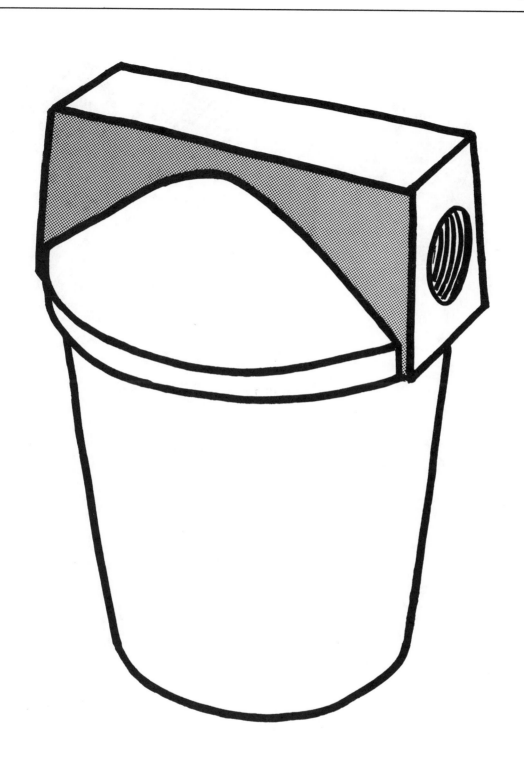

Geometrizing is an obvious thing to do, especially when the chosen manufacturing methods encourage it.

Figure 41

Even in purely organic forms, one discovers geometric organization when one decides to ignore variation of detail.

Figure 42

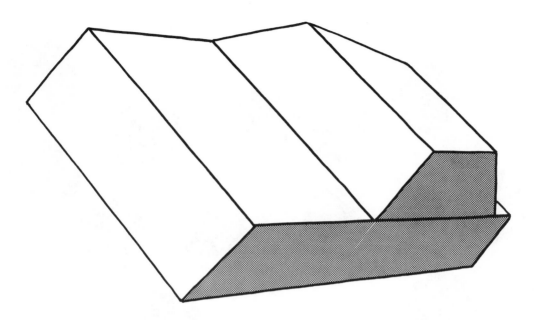

Similar to the shape of organic forms, the geometric plan of some industrial forms applies more to the general outline than to its final configuration.

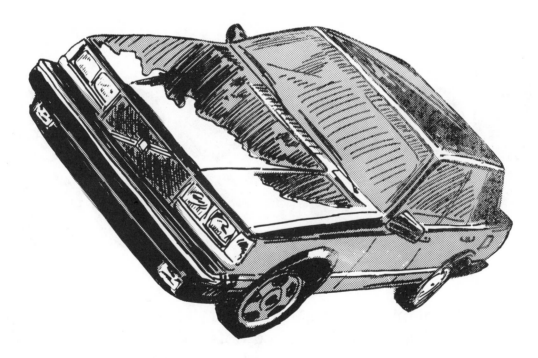

Figure 43

Reducing the number of visually relevant elements helps perception. Twelve chaotically distributed dots will make a more easily perceived pattern if they are grouped in two sets of six dots each.

Figure 44

58

A

B

C

D

The unity of the typewriter form is increasingly emphasized after each modernization, when the number of visually significant elements is reduced.

Figure 45

59

The evolution of the automobile shows the tendency to eliminate the number of visual elements without detriment to function. On the left is a design from 1928; on the right is one from 1962.

Figure 46

A 1987 design shows further elimination of individual visual elements. In this car, the lights are folded behind the front grill when not in use.

Figure 47

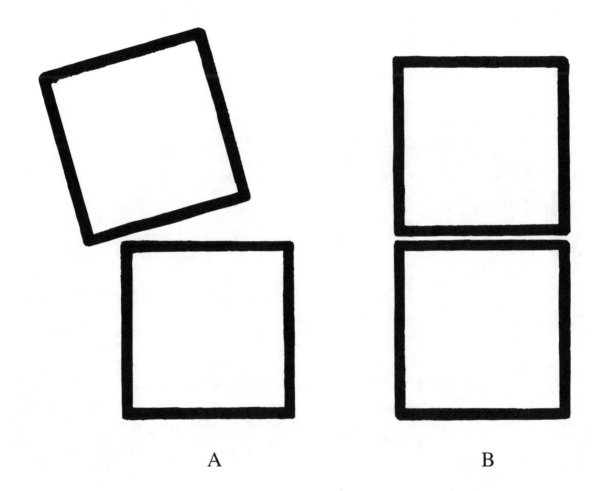

A   B

Compactness or cohesiveness of visual pattern facilitates perception. Out of two patterns made of the same components, the more
compact one is that on the right.

Figure 48

62

The tendency toward compact forms manifests itself in the preference for closed forms, which have a tight arrangement of elements, decisively separating from the environment the space they enclose or fill.

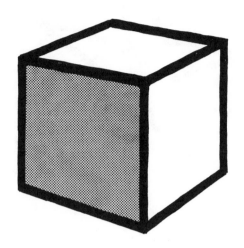 

Opposed to such organization are open forms with poorly defined borders between them and their surroundings and loosely connected elements, which can be interpreted ambiguously.

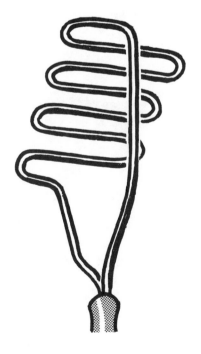 

Figure 49

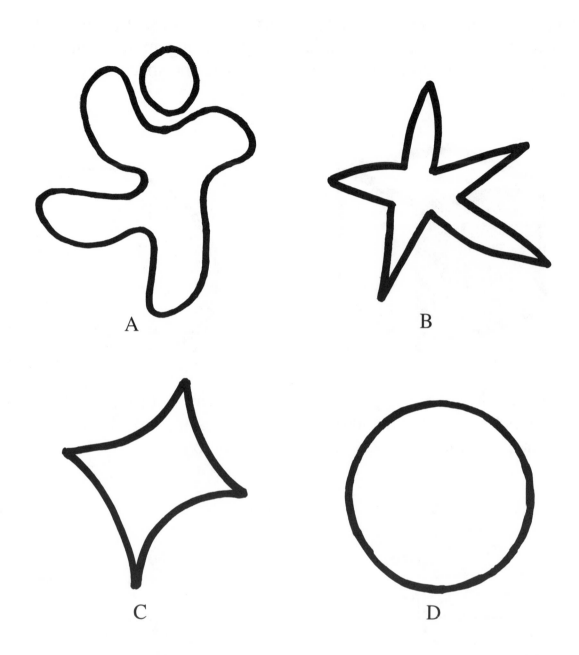

A

B

C

D

Compactness or cohesiveness can well be described as the ratio of the length of the form's contour to its surface.

When several forms are compared, the most compact is *D*, the one for which the value of this ratio is lowest.

Figure 50

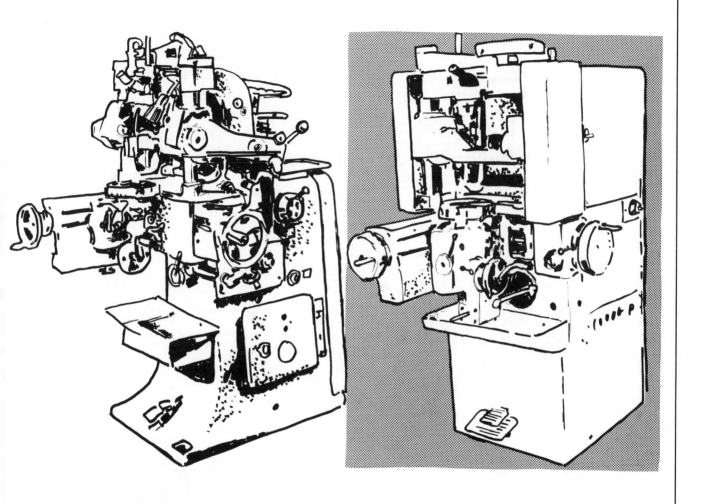

The tendency toward a compact form is seen in the development of this slotting machine.

Figure 51

The tendency toward compact forms is seen in the development of the automobile.

Figure 52

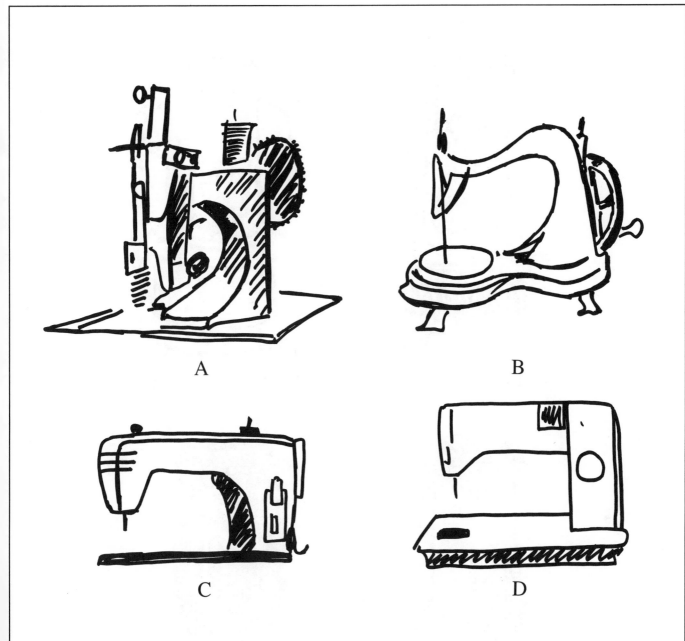

The tendency toward compact form in the development of the sewing machine…

Figure 53

67

A

B

C

D

…and the gas water heater.

Figure 54

A product designer may face a situation in which the product function makes it impossible to increase the cohesiveness of its form. This bicycle is a good example of such a product.

However, in general the utilitarian objectives of industrial products are well served by the application of organizing principles discovered by Gestalt psychology.

Figure 55

69

The tendency toward visual organization on a grid of straight lines manifests itself as a spontaneous tendency to search for straight lines in the field of vision and to arrange visual patterns along these lines.

There are numerous examples of its application in architecture...

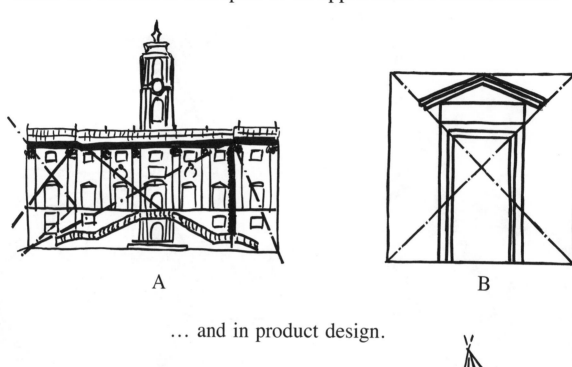

A

B

... and in product design.

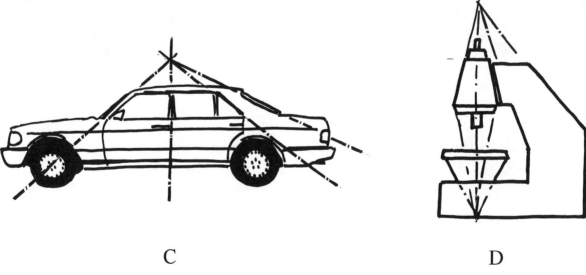

C

D

Figure 56

70

A modern motorbike. An example of a straight-line esthetic directive in the product's form, where there was none before.

The straight lines provide a sense of unity to the form. At the same time, the reference to the shape of a wedge suggests toughness and generates the appeal of an irresistible force.

Figure 57

71

The esthetic appreciation of purpose (value Y, fig. 27) yields only to that of visual order in its universal appeal.

The human body, exceedingly complex and at the same time an effectively simple combination of a multitude of control and executive components, is one of the first instruments to facilitate the assimilation of the laws of nature by our subconsciousness.

Figure 58

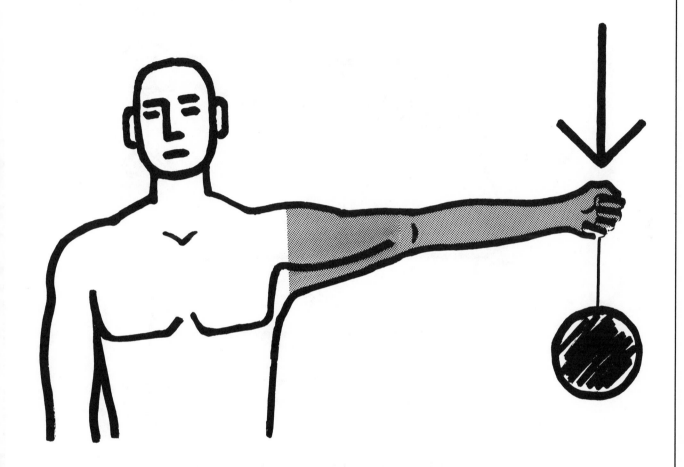

An arm is thicker at the shoulder than at the wrist; a force applied to a cantilever beam creates bending of the beam, which increases toward the point of fixation.

Figure59

73

The increasing bending requires the resistance of the growing cross-section of the beam.

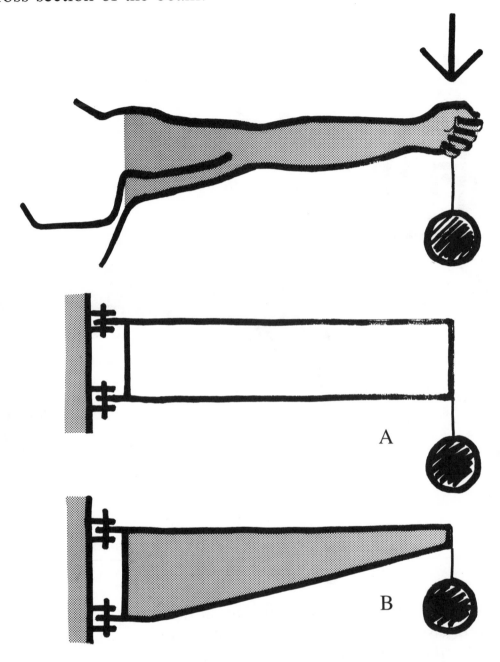

The appearance of crane *B* will most likely be judged superior to that of *A* since it better communicates the fitness of the beam to resist force.

Figure 60

74

Another example: standing with legs placed wide apart increases stability.

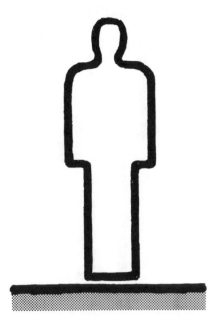 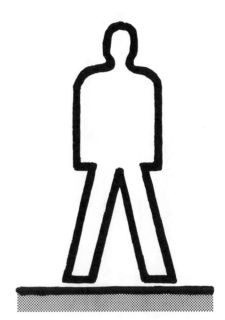

Interpretation: A wider base stabilizes the mass.

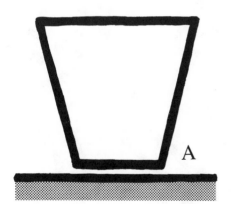 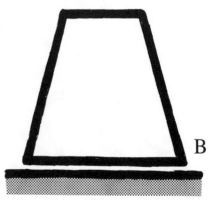

Which of the above masses will more likely appeal to someone in search of stability, *A* or *B*?

Figure 61

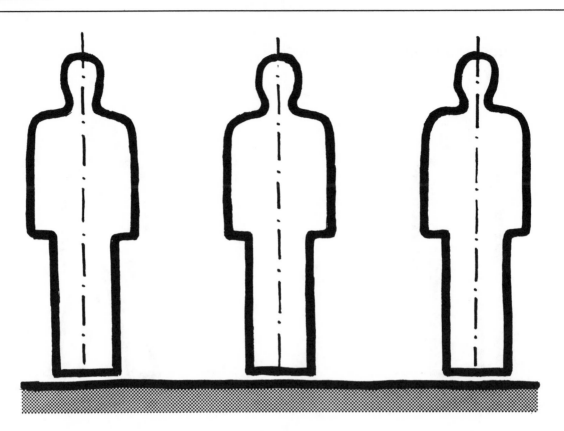

The vertical line implies an absence of movement.

The slanted line suggests movement.

Figure 62

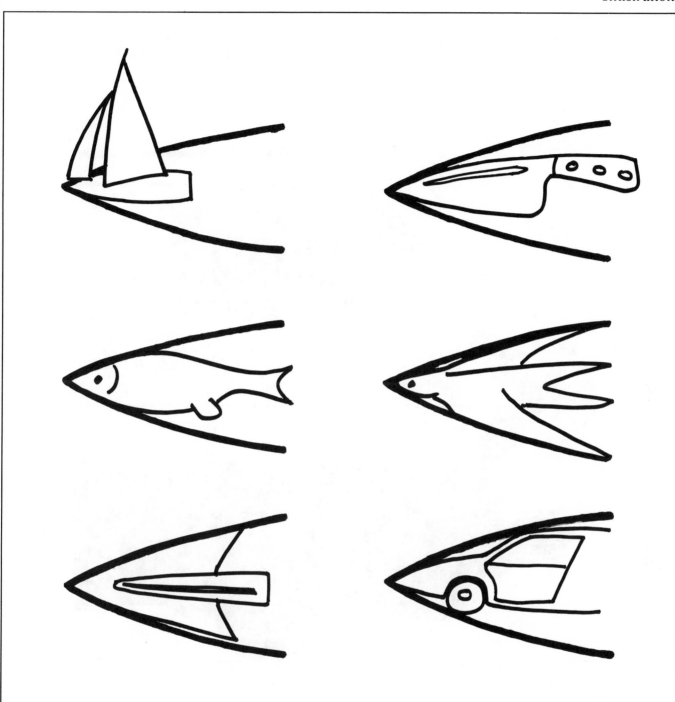

We learn purposefulness by observing the world around us. For instance, the function of movement is communicated well by the slanting lines meeting in the leading point of the moving object.

Figure 63

77

The use of the form of a wedge to express movement does not have to be explicit.

Sometimes just the suggestion of a wedge, as on this Canadian LRC high-speed train, improves the Y esthetic values of form functionality.

Figure 64

Information about the object is communicated through the application of specific classes of visual symbols.

Visual symbolism of

"inertia"
(low energy, sadness)

and "mobility"
(high energy, joy)

and their applications

Figure 65

More on the visual symbolism of

Inertia   and   Mobility.

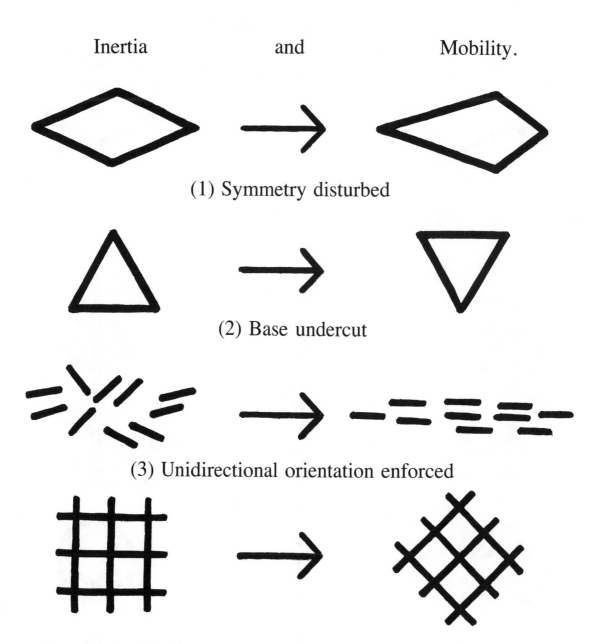

(1) Symmetry disturbed

(2) Base undercut

(3) Unidirectional orientation enforced

(4) Verticals and horizontals made slanted

Figure 66

Exercise: How to change the "slow" silhouette of a truck into the "fast" silhouette of a sports car?

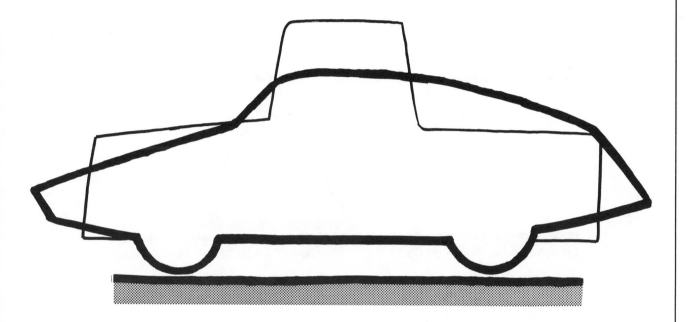

Using the visual means described in figure 66,

(1) The symmetry of the truck has been disturbed.
(2) Front and rear undercutting has weakened its visual stability.
(3) Horizontal elongation has emphasized the direction of movement.
(4) Horizontals and verticals have given place to slanted lines.

Figure 67

The visual communication of balance is another task frequently facing the designer.

In visual terms, "weight" is proportional to the size of the form.

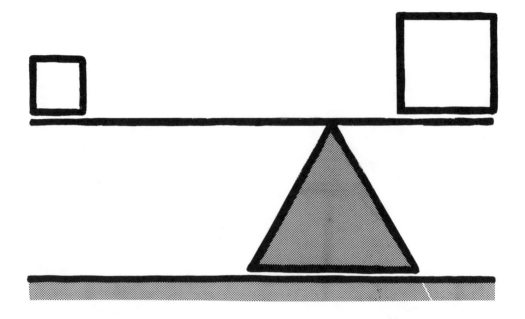

Black is "heavier" than white.

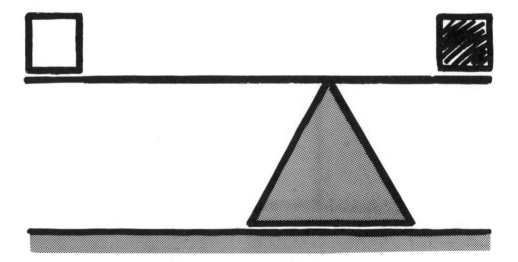

Figure 68

82

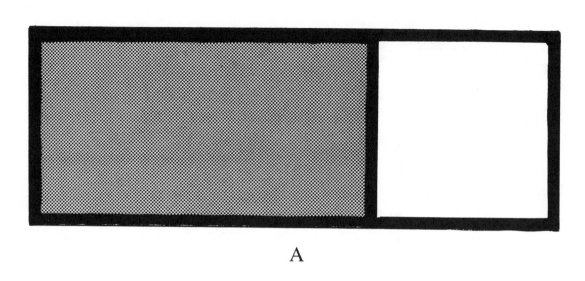

A

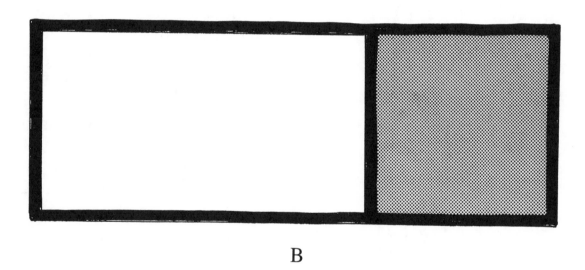

B

Unless other requirements of function override the need for visual balance, we will likely select housing *B* over *A* as the one better balanced.

Figure 69

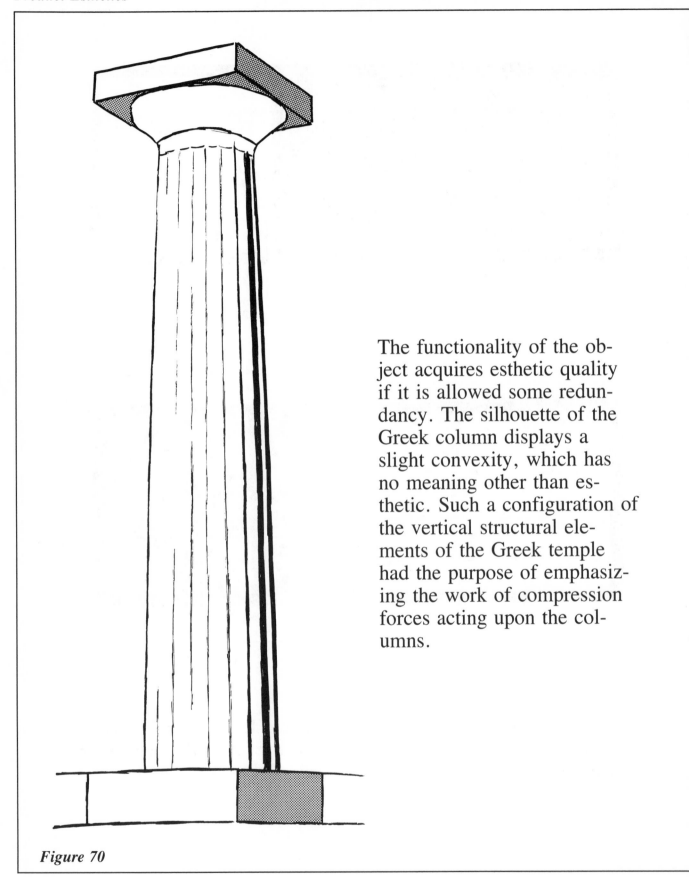

The functionality of the object acquires esthetic quality if it is allowed some redundancy. The silhouette of the Greek column displays a slight convexity, which has no meaning other than esthetic. Such a configuration of the vertical structural elements of the Greek temple had the purpose of emphasizing the work of compression forces acting upon the columns.

Figure 70

84

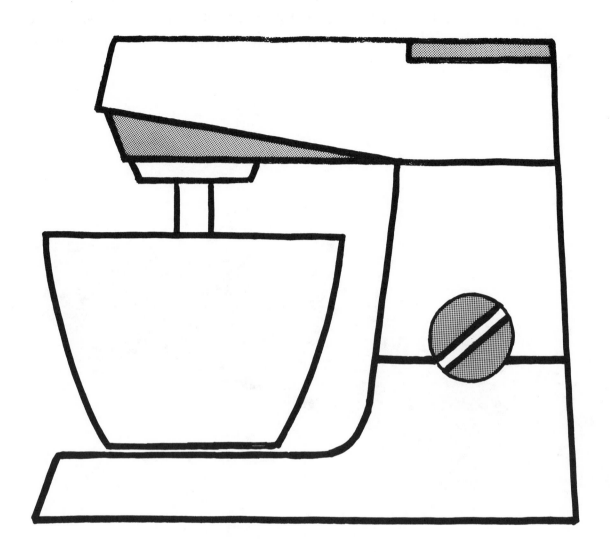

Function is emphasized by giving the beam of the mixer a beamlike appearance. In reality, the top and bottom surfaces are parallel.

Figure 71

The primary function of the molding on the side of the automobile is to protect the side when it comes into contact with minor obstacles.

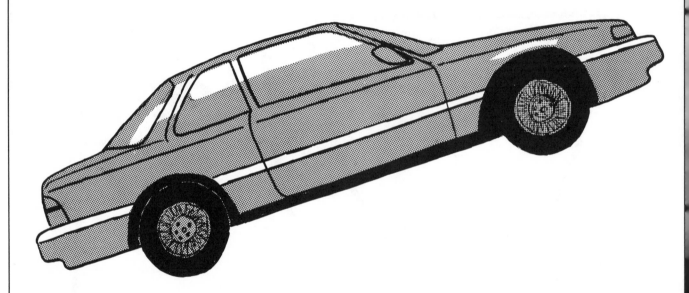

However, for this purpose the molding could just as well be visually blended with the car body. The deliberate contrast between the molding and its background has the purely esthetic objective of emphasizing the horizontal movement of the car (value Y).

Figure 72

86

At the level of Z esthetic values (ref. fig. 27), associated with fashion and taste, a prospective buyer of an automobile looks beyond the car's function as a means of transportation.

The choice of automobile tells a lot about the buyer, for instance, whether the buyer wants to project an image of "rugged, unconquerable individual"…

Figure 73

...or a "no-nonsense man of business"...

...or a "free spirit of the highway."

Figure 74

Designers add Z value to products' appearance by referring to cultural images that they consider appropriate and useful. For instance, in the field of industrial products there is a clear propensity for imitating the visual patterns associated with the leader in technology.

A car builder promotes a product by playing with the visual similarities between the appearance of the car and the space shuttle.

Figure 75

There is room for esthetic intervention even in the most technical assignments.

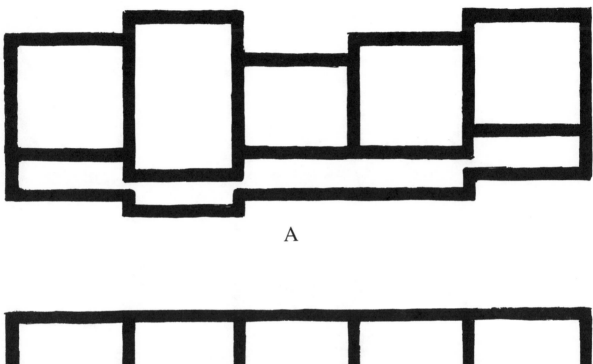

A

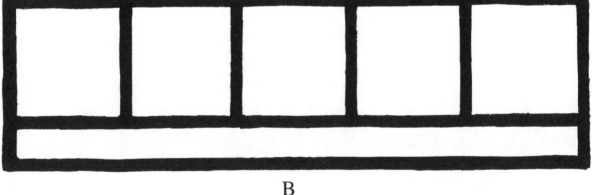

B

For instance, if the technically correct arrangement *A* can be modified without detriment to its function, such a solution will most likely be judged esthetically preferable. However, should the product of modification project a sense of visual monotony, the design process will continue.

Figure 76

On the other hand, the visual communication of function may require contrary measures.

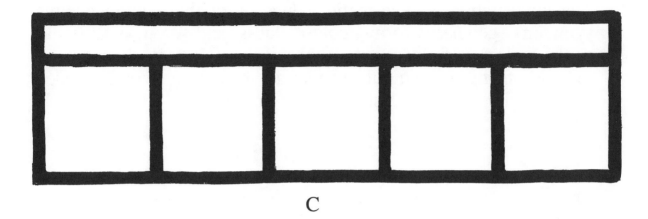

C

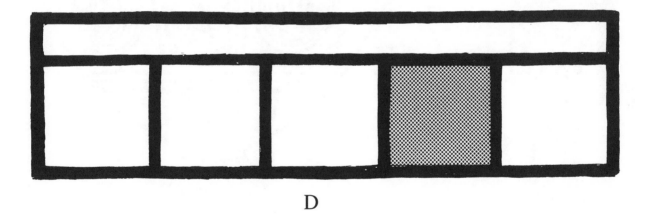

D

Suppose that form *C* fulfills the technical requirements. We may still notice a slight inadequacy of design, because the second square from the right has a special function but its functional uniqueness is not communicated. In such a case, a modification *D* might improve the esthetic appropriateness of the form.

Figure 77

Let us review the esthetic values of order, function, and culture (X, Y, and Z) by referring to a selection of actual utilitarian objects.

The appreciation of X esthetic values of rhythm, homogeneity, symmetry, geometric forms, cohesiveness, and so on, is as stable as the biological foundations of these values. In fact, there are no records of any meaningful changes in the structure of X values from the time of the oldest preserved artifacts.

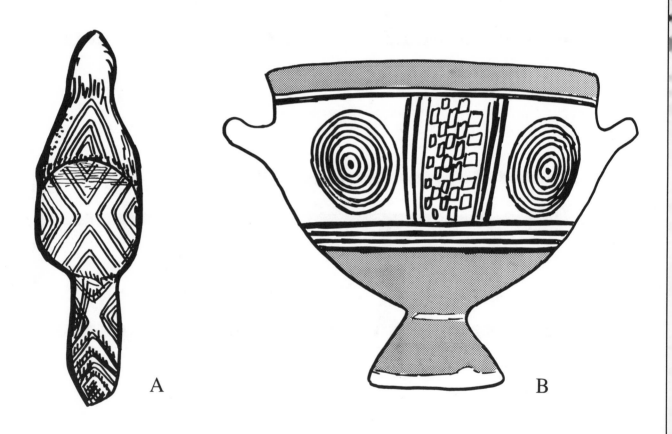

A A carving of a paleolithic toy bird, 20,000 B.C.
B An ancient Greek vase, 500 B.C.

Figure 78

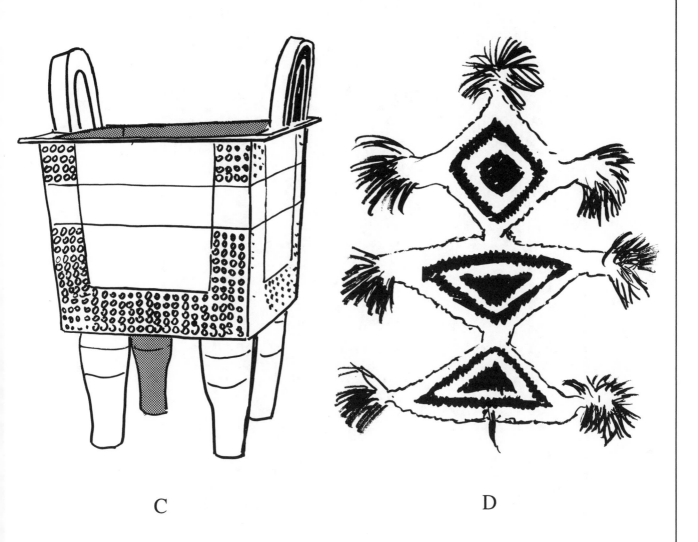

C   D

A Chinese cooking pot dating to 1,500 B.C. *C* and a contemporary Australian aboriginal cult artifact *D* both show a remarkable geometrical structure.

Figure 79

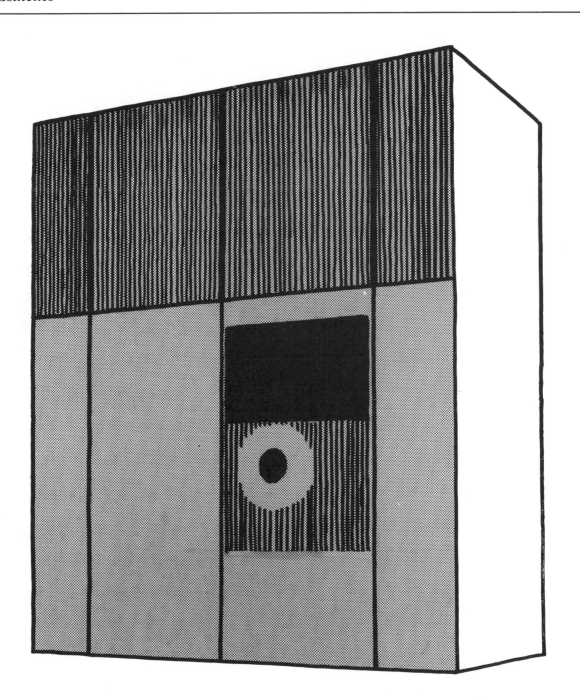

Computerized office equipment—an example of modern design idiom. Clarity and classical simplicity. Symmetry along the vertical center line and a "golden mean" (.618) division of height (see commentary 1.5.3)

Figure 80

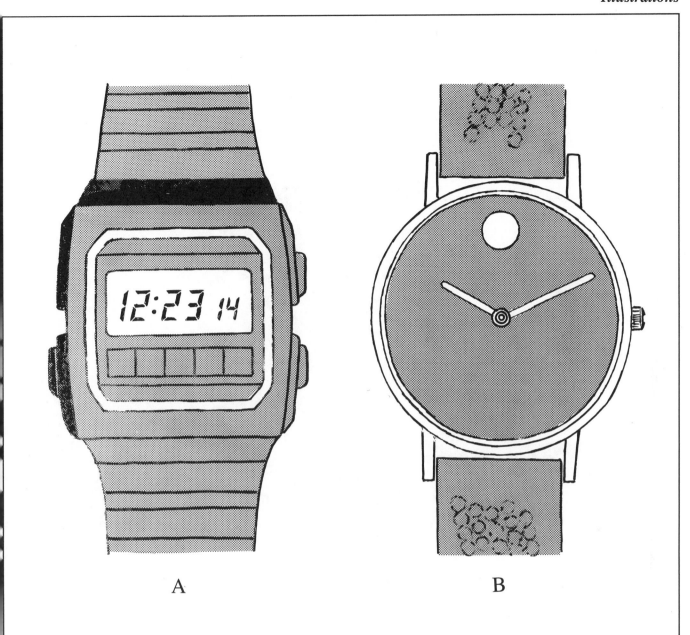

A   B

Modern wrist watches: the visual unity of *A* has been achieved by
emphasizing two main directions of lines and by enclosing the
smaller functional elements of the face within one clearly defined
border. Watch *B* displays symmetry, homogeneity of visual circu-
lar components, and an austere geometric structure.

Figure 81

95

The power of this four-wheel-drive agriculture tractor is visible in its purposely rugged design.

A clearly defined grid of straight lines conveys the sense of unity (value X). A slight forward tilt of the verticals increases the perception of a charging, irresistible force (value Y).

Figure 82

Esthetic appreciation of function (value Y) is not as widely established as that of visual order (value X). And yet, with a function as common as cutting, for instance, forms originating 6,000 years apart show a dramatic similarity of shape and visual beauty.

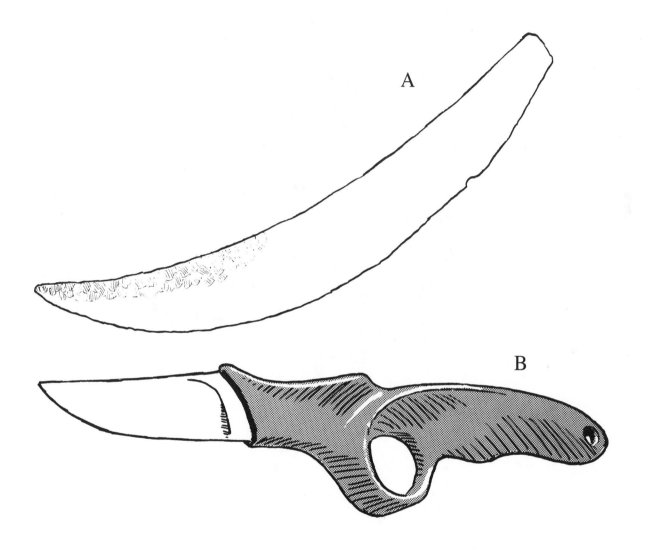

A Predynastic Egyptian stone blade, 4,000 B.C.
B Contemporary utility knife.

Figure 83

97

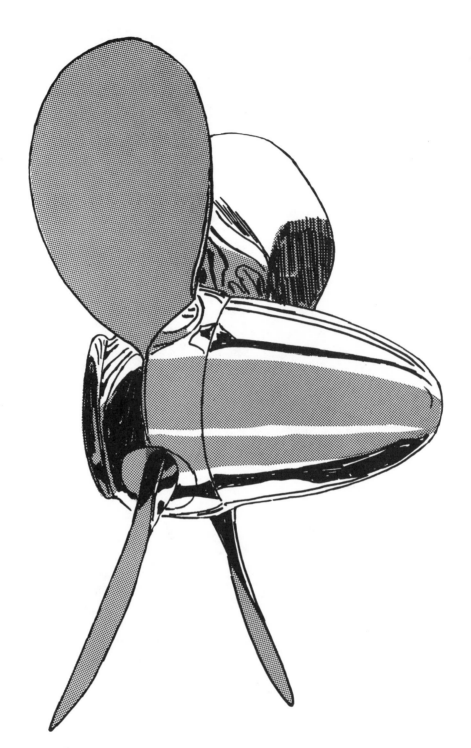

Purposefulness of form can be appreciated by humans who assimilate the laws of nature in everyday experience.

Figure 84

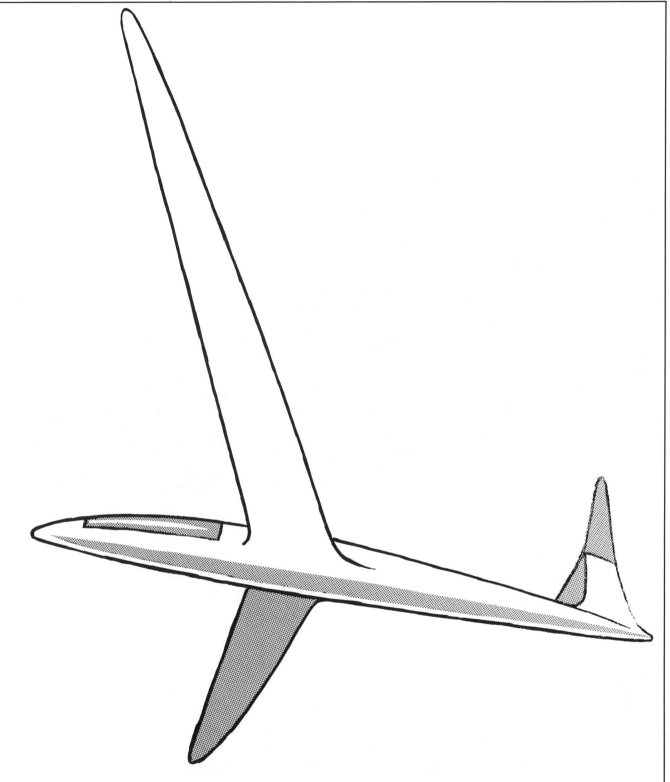

At least in part, instinctive appreciation of function shapes our enjoyment at the sight of a streamlined glider soaring in the skies…

Figure 85

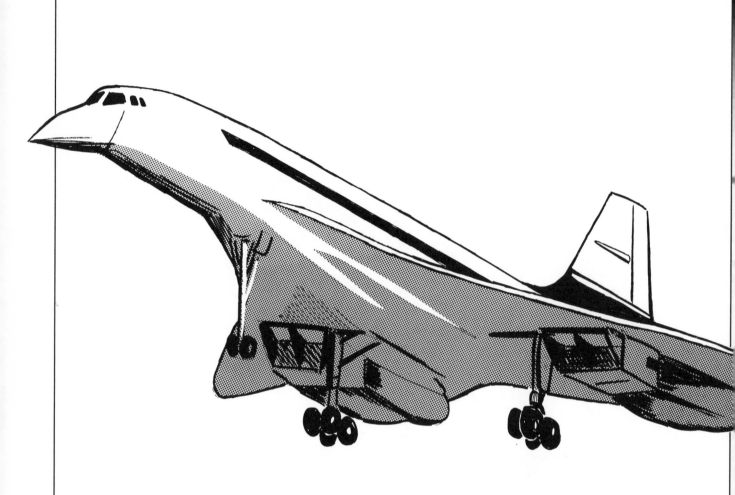

...and of a delta wing passenger jet, which is shaped the way it is to overcome the higher resistance of the air at supersonic speeds.

Figure 86

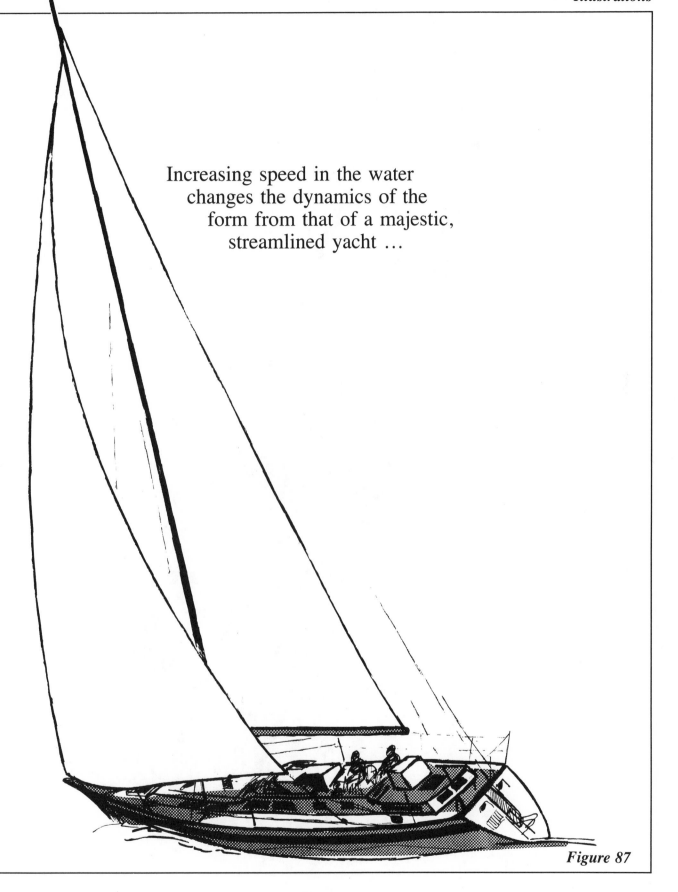

Increasing speed in the water
changes the dynamics of the
form from that of a majestic,
streamlined yacht ...

Figure 87

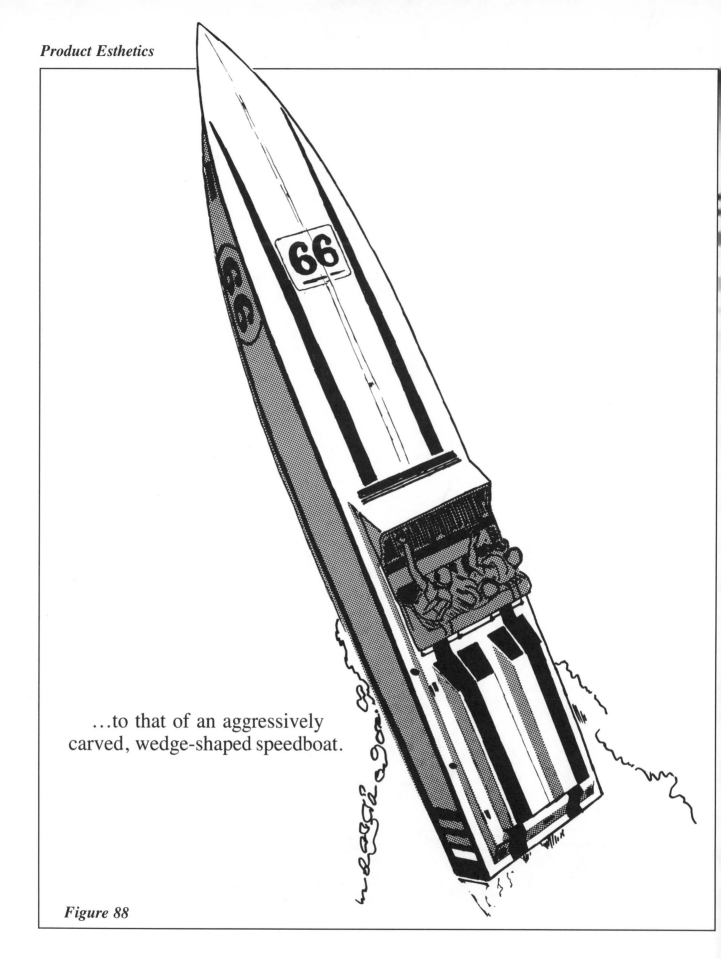

...to that of an aggressively carved, wedge-shaped speedboat.

Figure 88

Elongation of masses in the direction of movement provides an "excess" of functionality in the visual translation of motion.

Compare the application of the same means of expression in the native rock-painting in the Sahara Desert and the contemporary scooter (front fender!).

Figure 89

Even such an obviously inert mass as that of a motor yacht or an ocean liner can be graced through a subtle emphasis on the visual symbols of mobility: slanted lines of the geometric plan and the elongation of the front.

Figure 90

Organic forms ideally express the balance between the outside forces and the resistance of the form's material. The onlooker instinctively perceives and enjoys their fitness to the conditions of their existence.

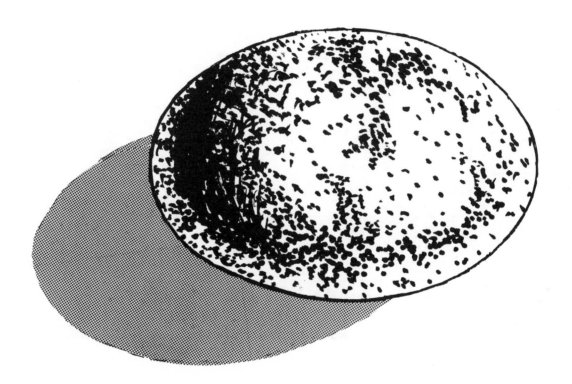

After being thrashed against the rocks and sand for millions of years, the oval surface of a stone found on the Ontario beach of Lake Superior has acquired the shape of the least resistance to those grinding forces.

Figure 91

105

Rather than being explicit, an image of an organic form may sometimes be merely suggested in the shape of the product.

A designer chose to project the compactness of a rock polished by sandstorms into the form of an office stapler. The cutout necessary for the function of stapling the paper does not greatly disturb the regularity of the esthetic directive of the form. We sense the existence of an invisible line running between the upper and lower jaws of the stapler.

Figure 92

106

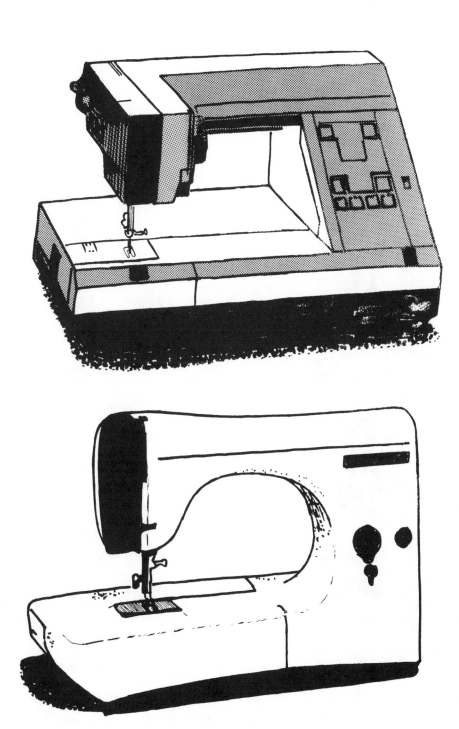

There is always more than one way of approaching a design as
shown by these two sewing machines, one crisply geometric, the
other clearly referring to organic forms.

Figure 93

Contrary to X values, Z values related to a temporary style or fashion show a great plasticity. At this level, esthetic preferences may change several times in one generation. Compare an Art Nouveau candlestick (late nineteenth century) with a contemporary one (on the right).

Figure 94

The influence of fashion is visible much more in the objects associated with leisure and luxury than those serving work and action.

Our style- or fashion-motivated preferences reveal the mystique and the individual character of the human self. For this reason we are less inclined to critically analyze the appropriateness of personal cultural values than those of visual order and functionality.

Figure 95

109

The look of the B-1 bomber generates awe. Is it because we react to the aircraft as a killer? Does the roar of its engines instill fear in our hearts? Is it because the bomber resembles a giant menacing bug? Is it because it is so big and fast? All our experience is conditioning our responsiveness to Z esthetic values.

Figure 96

110

A movable crane in action. A clear display of X and Y esthetic values, of visual order and functionality.

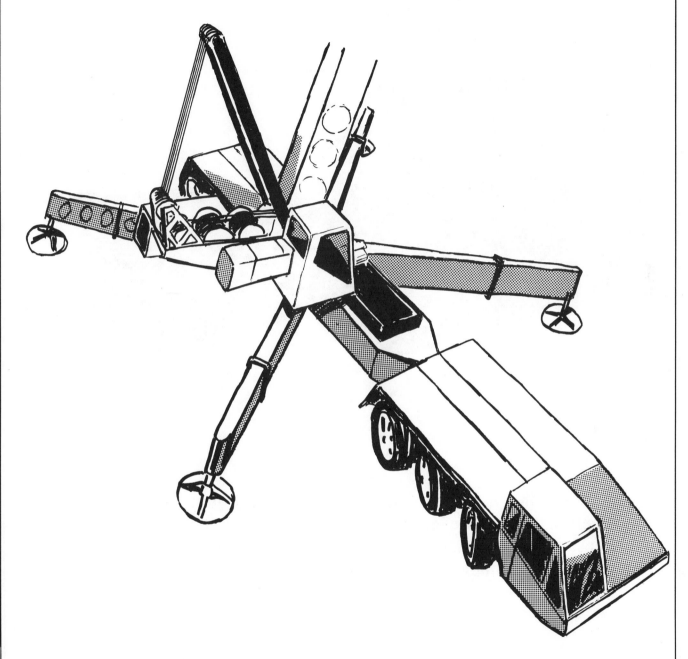

We may doubt whether, in this type of machinery, Z esthetic values, which relate to passing elements in the visual environment, will ever play a greater role.

Figure 97

As seen in this picture of a futuristic truck with a double-axle steering unit, however, a dramatic change in the look of heavy construction equipment is not inconceivable when new body-manufacturing technologies are introduced.

Figure 98

People intensely dislike boredom. Newly reshaped, repackaged products are welcomed every day, with an almost guaranteed market success. A surprise without a reduction of the product rationale will pay off. The tap above, in addition to having an attractive form, pours an unusual, bladelike stream of water.

Figure 99

113

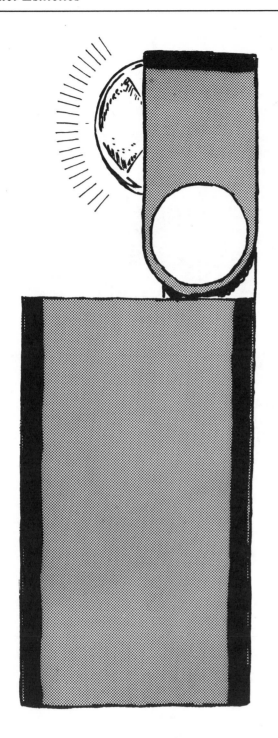

Now you see it, now you don't. A witty design for a flashlight surprises the customer and makes owning one fun. Humans always enjoy some degree of novelty and the unexpected.

Figure 100

The search for new, visually fresh products is partially satisfied by an innovative application of traditional materials, as in this coffee table...

Figure 101

115

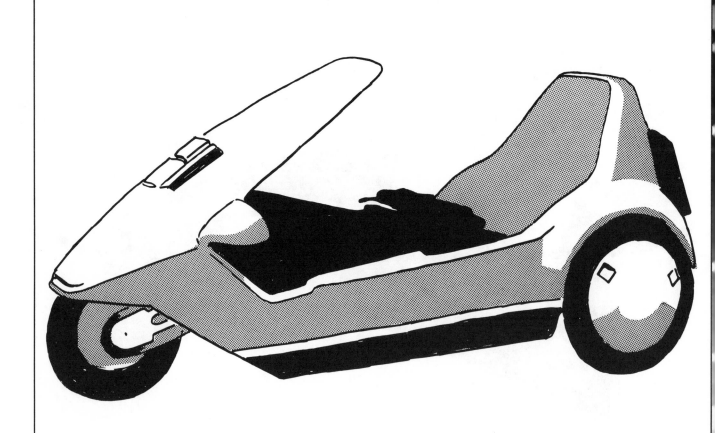

...and partially by the progress of technology. This pedal-assisted electric tricycle features an injection-molded polypropylene body and glass-reinforced nylon wheels.

Figure 102

116

Another example of a possible future electrically powered urban car with plastic body elements.

Figure 103

117

A modern telephone. Devoid of unnecessary details, the simplicity and clarity of form (X esthetic value) facilitates perception. The color-contrast of the base with the dial face and a receiver communicates well the functional importance of the latter (Y esthetic value).

Figure 104

118

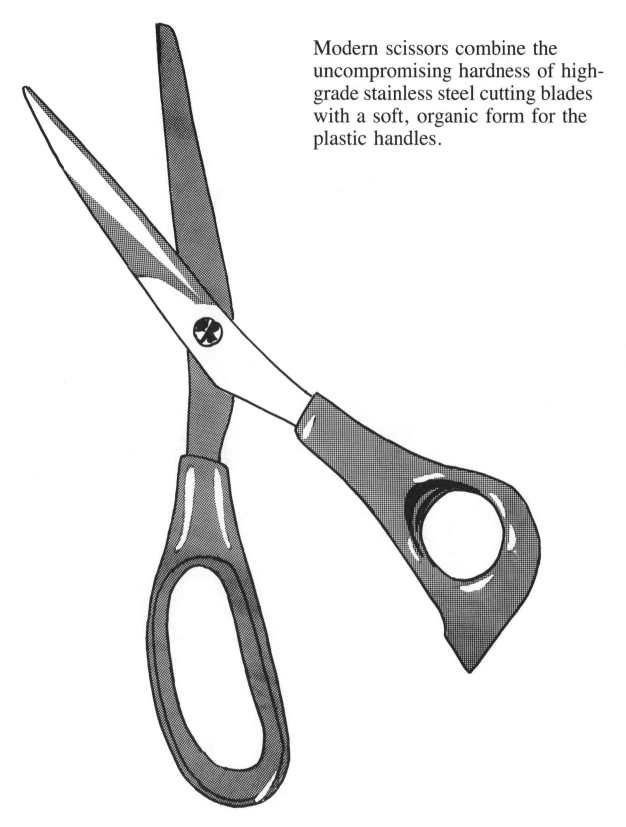

Modern scissors combine the uncompromising hardness of high-grade stainless steel cutting blades with a soft, organic form for the plastic handles.

Figure 105

A record player (top) and a radio amplifier are examples of modern industrial products.

The explicit cleanness and simplicity favored by some of the best designers have come to represent easily recognized components of the prevailing contemporary visual taste.

Figure 106

A modern photographic tripod displays the exactness and repetitiveness of applied manufacturing methods. The form conveys a sense of reliability, dependability, solidity—in a word, good quality. It did not take long before the precision of contemporary industrial forms came to be recognized as an esthetic value (Z).

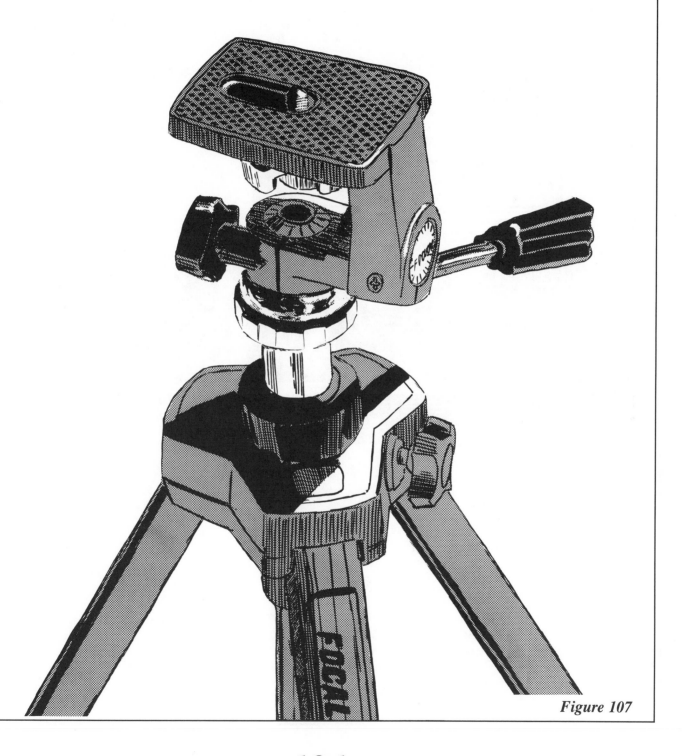

Figure 107

A portable personal computer is another example of a contemporary design emphasizing precision and exactness of detail.

Figure 108

One of the first cast-aluminum automobile wheel rims. X esthetic values: rhythm, homogeneity, symmetry, geometry. Y esthetic values: a radial arrangement of diamonds revealing the transfer of forces from the tire to the hub. Z esthetic values: direct exposure and display of modern materials and technologies. In addition, the design alludes subtly to forms originating in nature that are always well accepted. The center section creates associations with an exotic flower or a snowflake.

Figure 109

A modern taxicab. Verticals and horizontals predominate in this no-nonsense rational form emphasizing roominess and dependability. The wedge of the short hood adds a little spark to the design—a subtle dramatization of the form.

Figure 110

A modern, light-rail vehicle in the streets of San Francisco. Its attractive features are the result of its simple and clearly defined form.

Notice that a thin frame around the windshield unifies into one visually significant rectangular field all the subordinate details within the framing. A shallow arch—the top section of the frame— adds energy to the design. The windshield is wider at the bottom, projecting a sense of stability. The windshield divides the front of the vehicle in the golden-mnean proportion of 0.618 (see commentary 1.5.3).

Figure 111

The potential for a surprising and interesting design seems unlimited, even with the use of simple means of expression.

The front of the West Berlin mass transit S-Bahn vehicle.

Figure 112

An industrial form can grow only as far as the function of the product permits. Anything in the industrial form that extends beyond the technological rationale runs the risk of becoming ridiculous.

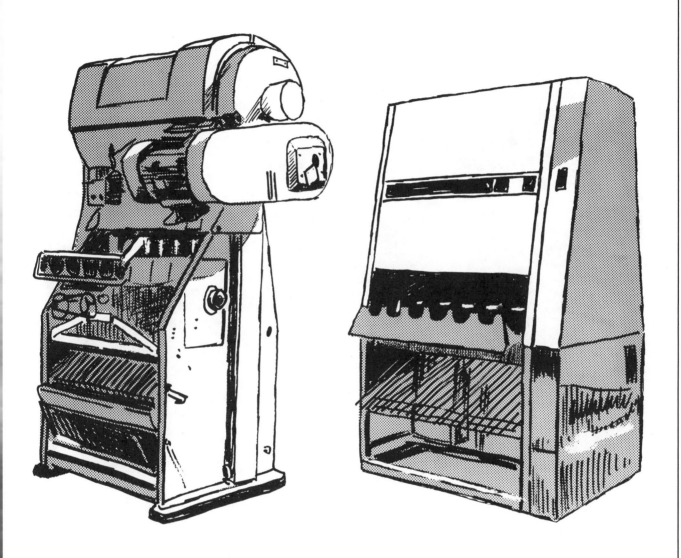

However, within the constraints of the function there is usually enough margin of freedom left to allow esthetic consideration in design, as seen in this modernization of an orange-processing machine.

Figure 113

A good product designer will strive for the optimum balance among the characteristics of the product.

This modification of a garden tractor not only brought an improvement of product appearance but also sizable direct gains to its manufacturer. The number of body parts was reduced from twenty nine to fifteen. The cost of components was cut by $100,000 per annum, 20% of the original cost.

Figure 114

A product-design process in which an esthetic objective is one of
the goals eludes attempts at easy characterization.

Figure 115

Creative pursuit governs itself with its own laws, of which the most prominent is the one requiring no restraining formulas in the approach to a design problem.

Figure 116

It is not inconceivable that the work may start not with definition of the function of the product and its technical characteristics but with an urgent esthetic vision.

A study of a conventional high-speed train for a proposed Los Angeles–Las Vegas corridor.

Figure 117

131

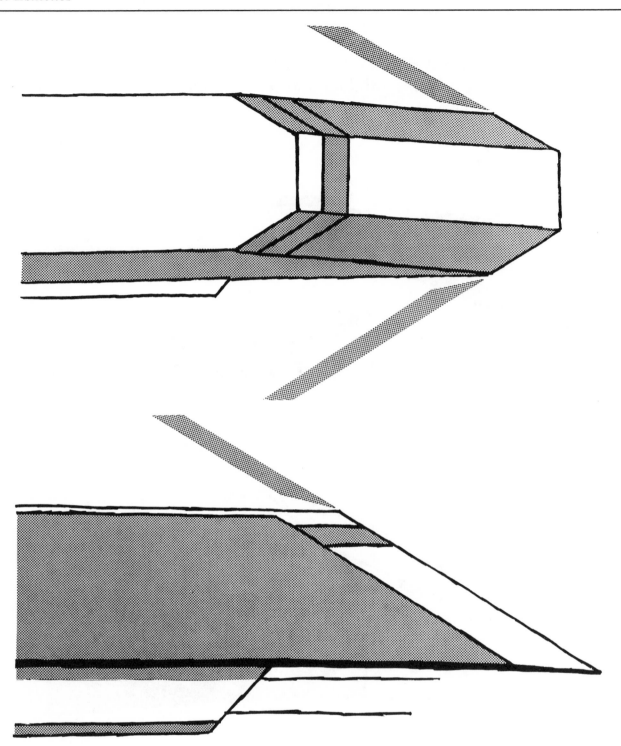

A study of a magnetic levitation high-speed train for a proposed Los Angeles–Las Vegas corridor.

Figure 118

However, the search for a particular visual quality usually starts with the laying down of the technical and operational requirements of the product. The design of a cargo truck proceeded as follows:

(*A*) The components of the truck and its typical cargo were laid down; (*B*) the main dimensions of the body were established; (*C-G*) the body was built around the components; and (*H*) the esthetic directive of the car body was an underframe "trough" emphasizing the function of carrying cargo. The concept of a "trough" played an essential role in a functional division of the car-body shell for the development of utility versions of the truck.

Figure 119

The final design of the truck described in figure 119.

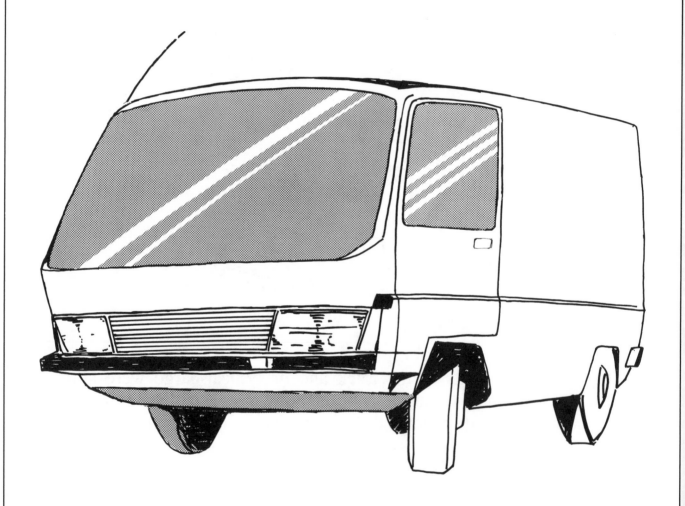

Figure 120

To prove the rationale of a design, the prototype is frequently built several years ahead of the first production unit. This is a 1987 running model of the Volkswagen "Golf," which will be built for the market, if ever, a number of years after the testing of this new design is completed.

Figure 121

135

When an esthetic goal was not neglected, a manufacturing study of a high-speed, self-propelled rail unit led to...

Figure 122

136

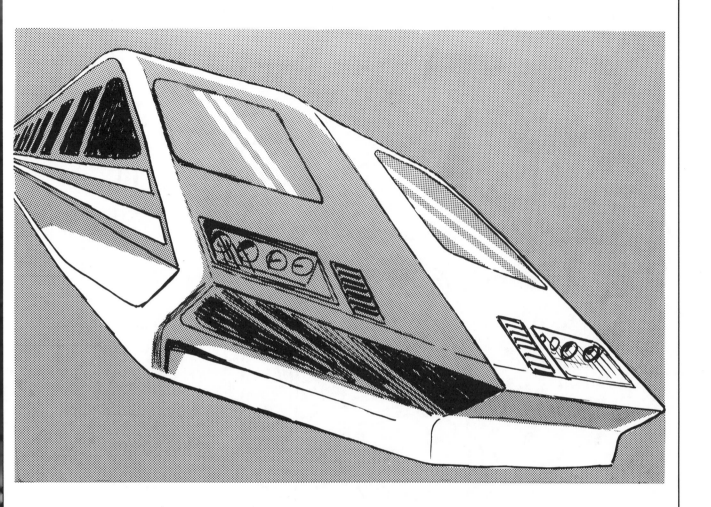

...design of an attractive form.

Figure 123

An assignment: A manufacturer of ski chair lifts planned to expand production and build a ski gondola. How do you use the existing parts and tools? Repetition of body parts was an asset.

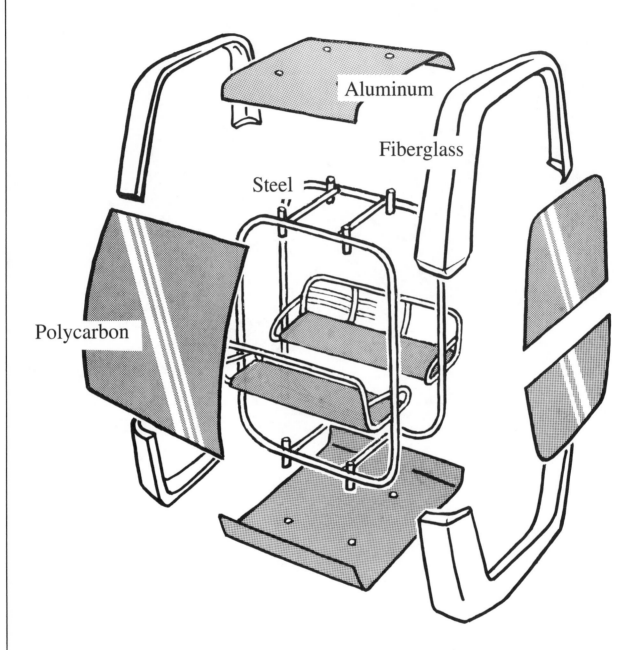

Solution: Join two triple-chair frames face-to-face, and apply sheathing to the frame.

Figure 124

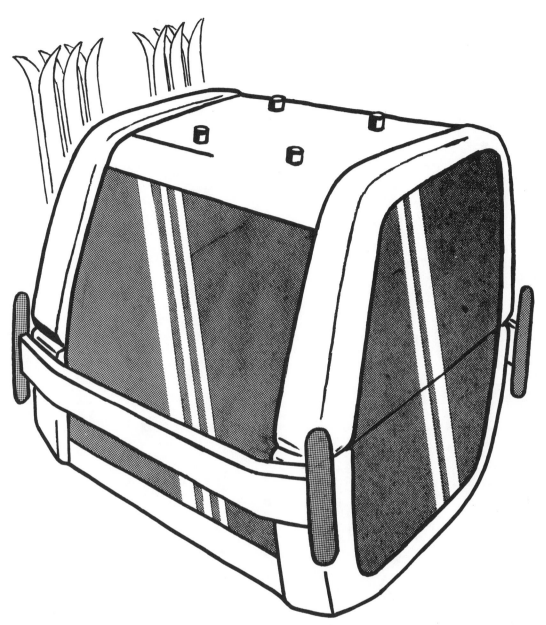

The development of a good product requires familiarity with its function, knowledge of materials and the way the materials behave under stress, knowledge of the methods and economy of production, and the application of the principles of human engineering. Esthetic quality further enhances the appeal of the product. This is because people prefer to live in pleasant surroundings. Attractive products make people happy, increase their efficiency, and contribute to their fulfillment.

Figure 125

139

Part

2

In

a

Capsule

Chapter 1. Terms Defined

1.1 Human Needs

Sources of information on the esthetic value of ordinary objects are scarce, but individual, energetically defended opinions on the subject exist in abundance. It seems only natural to start with an explanation of how some of the basic terms will be used. Accordingly, the first chapter will be entirely devoted to the examination of the terms for *need, form, beauty, expression, esthetic value,* and *esthetic emotion.*

Life may be seen as a perpetual adaptation of organisms to the surrounding environment. Human life is no exception. The necessities of life impose on us the continual effort of supporting the functions of our organism in a biological sense as well as on the economic and social scenes. The goals toward which our efforts should be directed are indicated through the emergence of needs.

The major premise of this book is that an industrial product will appear attractive if its form conveys the promise of fulfilling the needs of the onlooker.

The meaning of *need* is difficult to describe. For our purposes it will be enough to understand a need intuitively as something that requires compensation.

The whole body of needs oppressing or challenging humans was analyzed and classified by, among others, psychologist Abraham Maslow. Maslow's classification of needs can be represented in the form of a pyramid (fig. 1). The fundamental physiological needs are at the base, while the specifically human, spiritual need of self-actualization tops the pyramid.

In all, Maslow's hierarchy of needs has five layers, from the bottom to the top as follows:

1. Physiological needs, such as hunger, thirst, and sex drive.

2. The need for safety, security, protection from physical harm.

3. The need to belong, for love, affection, acceptance, and friendship.

4. The need for esteem from others and for self-esteem.

5. The need for self-actualization, for becoming what one is capable of becoming ("What one can be, one *must* be.").

Such a gradation of needs corresponds to the sequence for their usual compensation even though with certain individuals the need for self-actualization (for instance, the need to create) may prevail even over hunger. The narrowing range of needs toward the top of the pyramid represents their growing sophistication and therefore a decreasing number of individuals experiencing a given need. We may make the observation that while the lower needs are directed towards satiation, the higher ones seek production, creation, and growth of insight. Also, while lower needs are commonly shared, higher needs are highly individualized.

The expression "the user's needs" implies more than just the needs associated with the direct function of the product. The primary function of the automobile, for example, is to provide mobility. At the same time, the visual characteristics of its form may convey the promise of fulfilling other needs of the user such as the need of appearing to be a rugged, unconquerable individual, or a free spirit of the highway, or a no-nonsense man of business.

Shaping the form of the car body to communicate its primary function of providing a mobile shelter, caters to the desires that Maslow would most likely have placed in layer 2 of the pyramid: within the need for safety. Giving it a look of ruggedness, sleekness, or dependability gratifies the higher-placed needs to belong, for esteem and for self-fulfillment.

1.2 Form

We appraise the esthetic value of the industrial product by looking at it. What we see is the form of the product.

Few terms are as ambiguous as the term *form*. We will conceive our first approximation of its meaning by equating form with the shape of the product. This is obviously an imperfect approximation because it excludes such elements of the object's appearance as light and shade, color and texture.

The other time-honored definition of form describes it as an arrangement or order of parts. However, product designers intuitively feel that the process of developing industrial forms is more than just arranging their components into visually pleasing patterns.

We will be no more satisfied when approaching the problem of form from the manufacturer's point of view. Manufacturers sometimes equate the form with the body of the product, its housing, or its casing. Such an approach to a meaning of form could possibly be justified in respect to, let us say, a home refrigerator, but it creates more problems with complex products. Is not a computer's keyboard a part of its form? Are not the automobile's seats or dashboard parts of its form?

Clearly, the above definitions are not satisfactory for our purposes. To increase our understanding of the meaning of the term *industrial form* we will turn to the language of cybernetics.

The pivotal concept of cybernetics is that of the system. A system can be broadly defined as a set of elements and the relationships between those elements and their properties. In its abstract wording, this definition can be applied not only to such different industrial products as a typewriter or a lathe, but also to living organisms as dissimilar as an amoeba and a human. All of them are systems; the first are technical, the latter biological.

Systems affect the surrounding world or receive stimuli from it through specific gates, accordingly referred to as *external exits or entries*. As an illustration, the typical external entries of the biological system of the human organism are the nervous-system receptors of eyes, ears, nose, and tongue and the skin receptors. The latter register both the sensations of touch and of changes in external temperatures.

The exits through which the human organism affects the outside world are its muscle/operational complex, its sound-generating vocal cords and mouth muscles, its gates for disposing of waste, saliva, sweat, and reproductive cells and, finally, the characteristics of its appearance.

In the exemplary technical system of a radio, the external entries are an on/off switch, volume and tone adjusters, and tuning or selection adjusters. The external exits are the speakers, the monitor of a tuning scale, stereo indicator, and so on, and, again, its appearance.

Note that by adjusting the regulating knobs and levers of the radio, the operator changes the sound emissions of the speaker. The speaker emits an infinite selection of broadcasting stations, tones, and volumes, which enter the operator's biological system through the entry of the nervous receptors in the ears.

This loop of alternate causes and effects from the operator to the radio and back to the operator is called a *feedback loop*. Since this arrangement engages two systems, biological and technical, it is frequently referred to as a biotechnical feedback loop (fig. 9).

The ability to behave according to a feedback scenario is the property of all self-regulating systems (see, for instance, figs. 6 and 7). All living organisms, including humans, maintain a balance with their environments by employing the feedback principle (see fig. 8).

Feedback loops between human biological systems and technical systems are typical of the process of using industrial products. We will later show how esthetic emotion appears in the process of forming a feedback relationship between the product and its user and what its role is in maintaining the user's organism in balance with its environment.

Based on the above review of the terms of cybernetics, we may now present a definition of industrial form in its abstract sense:

> *Industrial form* is a set of external entries and exits of the technical system of the product which, in the process of the product's utilization, come into relationship with its user's biological system.

As this definition makes clear, the form of the product is the only channel through which the user can engage in a relationship with the industrial product (fig. 5). Note, then, that while designing the form, the product designer makes decisions about those external entries and exits of the product that come into biotechnical feedback relationship with the product's users. One of such a defined product's external exits is its appearance.

The relationship of this abstract definition to the material representations of industrial form is similar to that of the geometric definition of a circle to material representations of it such as a wheel, a round washer, and so on. Such a definition has several advantages:

1. It is broad enough to include the forms of all industrial products, irrespective of their functions or the manufacturing methods applied in their production.

2. It includes other, previously mentioned, narrower definitions of form.

3. The definition clearly labels appearance as only one of many properties of form, such as strength, weight, resilience, and its human engineering characteristics, all of which play roles in the product's utilization. It follows that while designing a product's form, a product designer goes far beyond merely addressing its visual qualities.

To facilitate writing I will continue at times to use the word *form* as a common synonym of *shape*. The context in which it is used will indicate the meaning intended.

1.3 Beauty

While trying to define the traditional terms of the arts, almost invariably we complain about their ambiguity. *Beauty* is one of those ambiguous terms.

In applying this term to design, the greatest problem stems from its being used in two general meanings, one broad, the other narrow. Such are the historical roots of the term that, in its broad sense, *beauty* is synonymous with *excellence*. It comes to us from ancient Greece. For the Greeks to call a thing beautiful was simply to designate it as being admirable, excellent, or desirable. A sculpture or picture could be "beautiful" but so could be a sandal, a sword, or any other artifact that was functional or useful. It was also natural to refer to truth or to morally admirable acts as beautiful. These phrases expressed an attitude of admiration for a thing well done, no matter whether that thing was a work of art, an object of practical use, or an element of human activity.

Our contemporary, everyday language inherited this broad understanding of the term *beauty*. It is not inappropriate for us to comment, for instance, about the high mileage of a car as "beautiful." We talk about a beautiful meal, beautiful wine, and so on.

There exists, however, a narrower understanding of the term, which equates beauty only with qualities that provide pleasure to the senses, especially to that of sight. In this sense the term *beautiful* is synonymous with *visually excellent*. This position has probably never been better expressed than by the thirteenth-century philosopher St. Thomas Aquinas: "The beautiful is that which pleases us upon seeing."

It is important to remember that for the purpose of this book only the narrower definition of *beauty*, that of appearance, will be equated with the esthetically positive quality of an industrial form.

Please note that within the duality of the term *beauty,* it is possible to have a thing that is simultaneously beautiful and esthetically repulsive. To give an example, some insects or earthworms can be genuinely perceived as beautiful by the biologist investigating their structure and life functions. In ordinary perception, however, their appearance will rarely, if ever, be considered to be esthetically pleasing.

The above example is not as remote from the main subject of our investigation as it may appear. It is not unusual for product designers to neglect or underplay the esthetic qualities of a product on the premise that the product is functionally beautiful. They would say it has an esthetic value since it is functionally excellent. They would refer to the principle "form follows function" as the justification for a programmed inertia in the active seeking of visual beauty.

There is a subtle connection between these two types of beauty, the functional and the visual, or, accordingly, between practical value and esthetic value. We will examine this connection several times in the context of the book. At this point we will merely indicate that what is considered visually attractive finds its beginning in what is excellent in other aspects of life. In addition, to gain the status of being attractive, admired, and sought after, the visual patterns must have a universal meaning or at least appeal to a significant segment of the population.

What I am leading to is that if, for instance, all of us were interested in the research concerned with insects, our society might develop esthetic preferences to shapes and textures expressing the biological excellence of these little creatures. If you are smiling cynically and incredulously at this idea, think about the current success of shapes and textures that originated in the computer and space industries. We have robotlike shapes everywhere—not only in shops and offices but also in kitchens, bathrooms, toy departments, fashion shows, art galleries, and so on.

1.4 Expression

The term *expression* primarily refers to the external manifestation of states of mind, to mental disposition, or simply to feelings. A feeling can be expressed through nonverbal as well as verbal communication.

One can communicate despondence, for example, by using the spoken or written word. However, the same state of despondence may be conveyed through prolonged silence, inert facial muscles, or eyes devoid of sparkle. In fact, the entire body can communicate depression by means of lifeless, slow-motion movements. The fashionable term *body language* refers to this type of nonverbal communication.

In theater or cinematography, the same unhappiness may be communicated by a "proxy": a picture of a gloomy, bleak landscape or somber music—another mode of nonverbal communication of feelings.

There is, of course, a great demand for means of nonverbal communication in the field of design. The usefulness of the product increases if its function is clearly visible. So grow its esthetic qualities. Let us take, for instance, the molding on the side of an automobile. Its primary function is to protect the side in minor collisions (fig. 72). However, for this purpose the molding could just as well be blended visually with the car body. The deliberate contrast between the molding and its background has the purely esthetic objective of emphasizing the dynamics of the car's form. This horizontal accent helps to express the function of movement in the car.

This is how the word *expression* is sometimes used: a function, the action of gravity, the flow of forces, and so on, are "expressed" in the good form of an industrial product. The origins of the term *expression*, its inherently psychological meaning, make for even more characteristic use of it in design vernacular. Designers frequently refer to industrial products in a way usually reserved for the description of relationships between humans. For instance, a dear friend of mine, Jacek Sokalski, an architect from Milan, Italy, was using the word *inviting* in describing a funnel-shaped entrance to a ski holder, which we once designed for a ski lift gondola cabin. Similarly, the front of the B-1 bomber (fig. 96) is "sinister." Such examples can be multiplied. At times in my analysis of industrial products I will be using the words *inform* or *communicate* and their derivatives, when this seems appropriate as an alternative to *express*.

1.5 Esthetic Value and Esthetic Emotion

These two terms are as inseparable as twin stars: *esthetic values* are those values of a form that generate *esthetic emotions*.

The general structure of emotions will be analyzed in chapter 2. The purpose of this section is to review briefly some of the major existing interpretations of each term. Even though esthetic value and emotion are intuitively understood, no definition of any of these terms enjoys a wider acceptance than any other. At best, efforts continue to name at least some of their components.

First, esthetic experience is the experience of an observer, a spectator. Esthetic values are the values of the visual characteristics of the form. Second, esthetic emotion emerges without reference to what is known about the object, feeding itself on what is seen. Esthetic emotion emerges before any experience or knowledge of the object can be accumulated. Third, esthetic emotion develops instantaneously. We either like the object at first sight or not at all.

Theories attempting to explain esthetic value and emotion are many and varied. Perhaps the oldest is the ancient "Great Theory," which explains visual beauty as the result of the pleasing proportions of the parts of a form or as the result of the size and quality of components and the relationships between them.

Modern Gestalt theory, in application to esthetics, can be seen as an extension of the "Great Theory," and its development and refinement. It seeks the value of appearance in the order of parts in a form and in such of their arrangements as may be conducive to clarity and simplicity.

Proponents of Associational Esthetics hold that esthetic emotion derives from the association of values. Accordingly, esthetic emotion is based on the connections the mind develops between observed objects. Because of these connections, the acceptance that the mind grants to one object is then passed to the other object, which carries some resemblance to the first one.

The Functionalist Theory also implies the existence of past experience in the development of esthetic emotions. According to this theory, the suitability of the object for its purpose is always sought when judging whether the object is liked or not. This, of course, contradicts the earlier established principle that in the contemplation of visual beauty there must be no conscious thought of practical purposes. The apparent conflict can be reconciled, however, by indicating that, with time the original conscious influence of purposeful suitability becomes unconscious.

I have jotted down this selection of esthetic theories as a starting point. The objective of the investigation that follows will be to simplify the picture for the purpose of design. For a start, it is intriguing to notice that the described theories seem to arrange themselves into two groups: those emphasizing visual order and clarity, the constant and more objective components affecting visual perception, and those giving more importance to the acquired esthetic responses and emphasizing what is variable or conditioned, i.e., the subjective side of our relationship with the object being observed. To the first group belong the Great Theory and the Gestalt interpretation; to the second, the Associational Esthetics theory and the Functionalist theory.

Whatever the process of explaining an esthetic emotion, no valid reason exists for approaching it as if it were structurally different from any other emotion accompanying human activities. To gain insight into the nature and character of this phenomenon we will now investigate the informational value of emotions.

Chapter 2. Esthetic Emotion as Information

2.1 Human Adaptational Activities

The essence of life processes is the maintenance of the inner activities of the organism in agreement with outside forces. Life requires that changes in external conditions be followed by a modification of internal balances. This is the norm for all types of relationships between the human organism and its environment.

The indication that a disturbance of balance has occurred is the emergence of needs. We learned already that the elementary needs are either physiological or those of safety, love, esteem, and self-realization. The adaptational activities directed at the satisfaction of human needs are controlled by the nervous system. The nervous system governs the wide spectrum of adaptational activities, from simple to very complex.

Representative of one end of this spectrum are, for instance, activities that control the constant temperature of blood. These are relatively simple. On the opposite end might be, for instance, the actions of a politician running for Congress. All of these activities and many more are controlled at the same time from one control center! The secret of this possibility lies in the extensive automation of the system. The nervous system is able to handle new and complex situations only because simpler and routine operations are fully automated.

We will carefully examine this automatic, involuntary side of human behavior. I believe that esthetic emotions are one of the manifestations of these automatic processes of adaptation.

For a start, let us notice that despite many modes of behavior there exist the same three sequences in every reaction of an organism to stimuli from the environment. For instance, these sequences describe both the maintenance of blood temperature and behavior typical of political bargaining.

Sequence 1. Stimuli coming from the environment are received by the terminals of nerve fibers, the receptors. Then, the impulses carry the information about the environment along the nerves to the brain and spinal cord control center.

Sequence 2. This information is further analyzed as to its importance to life processes. The analysis leads to a decision about the organism's behavior in a given situation.

Sequence 3. The decision, encoded in nervous impulses and transmitted along nervous fibers, activates executory organs of the organism, the effectors, examples of which are muscles and glands. Effectors execute the adaptational activities of the organism.

As a result of these activities, the organism finds itself in a new situation. Information about this situation further shapes its consequent adaptational activities. This process provides a classic example of a feedback loop.

It is worthwhile to review once more the mechanics of a feedback loop, which we discussed in section 1.2 of chapter 1. The governor of Watt's steam engine is used here as an illustration because of the classical clarity of its interdependences.

The governor consists of two weights at the ends of free-swinging arms, which are attached to the opposite sides of a rotating shaft (fig. 6). As the speed of the engine increases, centrifugal force causes the weights to fly away from the shaft to which they are attached. This outward movement of the weights automatically narrows a throttle valve, which reduces the intake of steam and thus slows down the engine. If the engine goes too slowly, the weights drop, widening the throttle opening, and the speed of the engine is increased. Thus, every departure from the desired speed sets in motion the forces that tend to correct that departure. It is in this way that the numerous balances within living beings are maintained.

Figure 8 shows feedback dependencies for the regulation of carbon dioxide in the blood in a schematic form that compares to that of Watt's speed governor (fig. 7). Figure 9 illustrates a typical feedback between biological and technical systems.

2.2 From Simple to Complex Psychological Processes

We have already learned that a feedback activity loop is an elementary unit of each adaptational process. In order that we may better understand what is happening "inside us" to determine our choices, esthetic choices included, let us now identify the entire field of processes occurring in the nervous system. This we will do in a much-simplified way. We will briefly describe six examples of adaptational situations, examining the varying presence of subconsciousness, consciousness, emotions, and rational thinking in these situations (fig. 13).

The examples below have been arranged in an order that moves from relatively simple cases to those of greater complexity.

A. A feeling of discomfort in the wake of falling barometric pressure is the result of a physiological stimulus, which, running from baroreceptors through the nervous system, does not reach the level of consciousness. A feeling of unpleasantness emerges seemingly by itself. A person subjected to it perceives neither the stimulus causing the mild anxiety nor the process of analyzing it and making decisions as to the proper response to it: an accelerated breathing. The analysis that takes place in the nervous system is totally automatic. Consciousness receives only the final result: a feeling of discomfort.

   This is an example of one of the fundamental processes of maintaining the balances of an organism. Let us examine a slightly more complex situation.

155

B. The retraction of a hand as the result of getting burned is accompanied by the unpleasant feeling of pain. In this case, the pain and the negative emotion that follows are registered by the consciousness. However, the decision-making process leading to the withdrawal of the hand is, as in case A, spontaneous and does not engage the consciousness.

In the next example, let us further complicate the matter.

C. The cry of an animal being chased triggers in the hunter a physiological reaction, which mobilizes him for action. In the hunter's consciousness this reaction is felt as a strong agitation. In this case also, the process that leads to mobilization takes place outside of consciousness. It is so rapid that consciousness registers only the opening stimulus and the emotion immediately following.

D. An experienced machinist removes and discards a dull turning tool after only a couple of turns of the lathe. This action is preceded by the emergence of an emotion of dissatisfaction about the poor quality of the work. The process of reaching a decision takes place through the comparison of incoming pictures of a poorly done job with some expectations based on previous experience. In this case we have an example of sensory-motor thinking that is the result of the flow of overlapping perceived objects and situations in the consciousness. Sensory-motor thinking is typical in the execution of practical activities. Here, the content of perception is the subject of the analysis. However, the analysis itself develops in accordance with ready-made schemes and is automatic, unnoticed by the consciousness.

E. An investigation of the reason for an automobile engine stalling is an example of a series of complex situations and the relevant emotions of expectation, hope, and disappointment. In this case, the process of reaching a decision has the character of concrete thinking.

F. Abstract thinking in the course of establishing the ability to repeat test results can be an example of the most complex activities of analysis and assessment. Thinking of this type is usually associated with a high level of emotion.

As indicated earlier, the following sequences of the adaptational processes must *always* have occurred in the above cases.

— The sequence of receiving information

— The sequence of the analysis of the information and of decision making

— The sequence of the reaction of the organism to the analyzed situation. Emotion blends the process of evaluation with the activities of reaction.

The three main sequences (input, analysis, output) of all the discussed cases, from *A* to *F*, are represented graphically in figures 14 and 15. The diagram in figure 15 dramatizes that the emergence of a weaker or stronger emotion is an indispensable element of each of the analyzed situations, whereas the activities of evaluation and decision making may not be registered consciously at all. In human life the majority of activities are involuntary and controlled from the subconscious.

2.3 The Human as a Self-regulating System

By this time, a reader with some technical background should no longer be guessing. The described patterns of adaptational situations clearly resemble the processes occurring in the control circuits of "thinking machines"—computers. Specifically they apply to the input-analysis-output pattern of behavior. It is a similarity that originally occurred to the father of the theory of information and computer science, the mathematician Norbert Wiener, and his collaborators. While choosing the name of a new discipline they were about to found, they successfully introduced the name *cybernetics* (from the Greek *kybernetikos*), referring to the process of controlling systems, be they living organisms, machines, or societies.

The analogy between the human nervous system and the electronic circuit of a computer will be very helpful in our examination of how humans think and act. We may compare a human's control circuit to that of an autopilot. An autopilot is a machine that controls modern aircraft during long, boring flights and helps save pilots' energy for more complex operations. Despite variations in wind patterns and violent vertical gusts, the autopilot senses any changes and automatically corrects the position of the controls, unerringly leading the aircraft to its destination.

Similarly, most adaptational responses of human organisms are automatic. An example of such a response is what physiology refers to as a *reflex*. A reflex is an involuntary response of the organism to a stimulus. The formation time of such a response has been shortened and the response rendered automatic as much as possible.

The reason for the dominance of reflexes in the activities of the nervous system is economic necessity. The economics of life require that, proportionate to the importance and frequency of the stimulus, the response of the organism must be the fastest one possible. Reflexes are nothing more than the most useful behaviors in a specific life situation. They are responses of the nervous system, according to the patterns stored in the memory.

For instance, in the previously discussed case A (section 2.2), the deterioration of environmental condition (drop in barometric pressure), subjectively experienced as a discomfort, leads immediately to the effective defensive reflexes of the organism: an acceleration of breathing and a slowing down of physical activities. In the case of getting burned (case B), the first, most effective action is the immediate removal of the hand from the dangerous location.

Cases A and B, shown in sphere I in figure 15, belong to the large group of the most elementary inborn reflexes and are typical of all members of a given species. They are called *unconditioned reflexes*.

The significance of reflexes has been recognized by, among others, Russian physiologist Ivan Pavlov. In his famous experiment, Pavlov blew food powder down the throats of the dogs and observed the unconditioned reflex of secretion of saliva from salivary glands.

Unconditioned reflexes develop and consolidate in the process of natural selection. Natural selection favors the evolution of those specimens whose patterns of behavior are the most conducive to supporting life in given environmental conditions. Those specimens transfer the characteristics of their behavior to succeeding generations. Evolutionary branches die out whose behavior is not advantageous to the development of the species. The natural process of directing evolution toward the most useful changes is very slow, but the resulting structures of form and behavior are very stable.

The patterns of behavior stored in the memory of the nervous system may be compared to programs stored in the computer that controls the autopilot. Both perform similar functions. In response to changes in the environment, they actuate the effectors of the systems they control, thereby restoring a temporarily unsettled balance.

A great feature of computer-controlled systems is that, when our requirements of their work change, the programs that govern their behavior can be modified. The analogy between the human nervous system and a computer extends to this property also. The human nervous system has the ability to modify the patterns of reflexive responses within its life span. In fact, in practical terms not even that much time is required. Learning useful, new involuntary responses may be accomplished in a matter of days, hours, or even seconds. This facility greatly enriches human behavioral patterns and adaptational abilities.

Ivan Pavlov investigated some of these acquired automatic responses, which he called *conditioned reflexes*. They well describe the processes of learning, of changing habits and preferences, and of enriching the stock of stimuli that have significance for humans.

The classic Pavlovian experiment illustrating the process of acquiring a reflex proceeds as follows. A dog salivates while eating. If a bell is rung when serving the food, the dog salivates at the mere sound of the bell after some number of such associations between food and bell. Salivation has become a reflex conditioned by the stimulus of sound. Before conditioning, the inborn reflex of salivation occurred at the direct presence of food. After conditioning, the acquired reflex of salivation occurs at the sound of a bell. What is significant is that the new reflex can be conditioned to any stimuli that the dog recognizes, to all types of sound, smell, touch, and visual patterns.

The process of conditioning greatly increases the chances of survival for the animal. Through conditioning, the dog becomes responsive to a whole new range of stimuli significant in the search for food and in the avoidance of danger. A dog that has been beaten once will run away at the very sight of a stick. The link of purpose between the sight of a stick and the anticipated pain has developed into the defensive reflex of retreat.

Similar patterns occur in the conditioning of human reflexes. For example, before crossing the street we estimate the danger of being struck by vehicles, and we do so by assessing their speed and direction. After some practice, crossing the street becomes fully automatic. Catching the sound of an on-coming vehicle is enough to make us jump quickly toward the sidewalk—without losing time on an analysis of the situation. Our hasty retreat is associated with a negative emotion of annoyance or irritation. What has taken place is the reinforcement of the conditioned reflex of muscle activity at the moment of our leap toward safety, which is our response to the sound of the engine—an acoustical stimulus.

In the examples of a hunter and a machinist discussed earlier (cases C and D in sphere II, fig. 15), their quick, automatic sequences of behavior may have occurred because of earlier conditioning.

Conditioned reflexes play the same role as unconditioned ones. Both types of reflexes make the organism respond assimilatively to stimuli that are beneficial to it. Responses toward harmful stimuli are modulated negatively. In other words, both unconditioned and conditioned reflexes protect the existence and well-being of the organism. However, the ability to transmit the meaning of an unconditioned stimulus to a conditioned stimulus makes the conditioned reflex a much more subtle and universal tool for protecting and furthering human goals.

Some of the physiologists who continued Pavlov's research emphasized the role of rewards and punishments in learning behavior and called it, accordingly, the mechanism of positive and negative reinforcement. In the conventions of this concept, the dog reacts positively to the ringing of the bell because that sound promises something good—a reward, a serving of food. Similarly, the cry of an animal generates the hunter's excitement at the anticipation of the coming rewards: a kill, a trophy, meat and fur. The sight of a poorly machined part is associated with punishment for inferior performance; the dull tool is quickly replaced.

The process of acquiring automatic responses is a regular, everyday occurrence in relationships between human and environment. According to some psychologists, we learn effective behavior through a never-ending series of rewards and punishments. For humans, as equally important as biological stimuli are those stimuli of a technological, social, or cultural nature.

Activities that occur regularly, such as breathing, maintaining body balance, and performing habitual tasks (such as reaching for a glass of water or driving a car) are either inborn or learned, but all are fully automatic, i.e. reflexive. How many times have you solved a difficult design problem while driving home from work? You can think about other problems while driving (and I implore you, don't do this anymore!) because your driving responses, after a period of learning, no longer engage your awareness.

Of course, we use our brain for making significant decisions in our lives, or at least we should. However, in terms of sheer number, automatic responses controlled by impulses coming from the subconscious have a dramatic advantage over those controlled rationally.

2.4 Emotion as an Indicator of Value

While describing some selected adaptational situations, we referred to two distinctly different groups of occurrences. One group is made up of phenomena that can be observed from the outside, measured, and placed on record. Accelerated heartbeat, increase in blood pressure, muscle tension, and many other reactions belong to this group of occurrences. Pavlov, in his experiments with reflexes, was interested only in these types of phenomena. The time lapse between the sound of the bell and the start of salivation could be determined precisely. The amount of saliva secreted could be measured.

There is, however, another, quite different group of phenomena. We described this group with words such as *anxiety, elation, depression, joy, disenchantment, hope*. A common name for these psychological phenomena is *emotion*.

The term *emotion*, even though commonly, intuitively understood, is difficult to define. Emotion is said to be the animation of psyche, an enlivened state of mind, or a state of mental agitation.

The difficulties of describing emotion are equaled by those of dealing with emotion as a subject of scientific investigation. A direct way to learn about an emotion is through an examination of the evidence given by a person who is experiencing that emotion. The quality of such a description depends on the ability of a person to communicate, not on the accuracy of the scientific instruments. This is why Pavlov and the psychologists who continued his work had no use for the emotions at all. Emotion was entirely outside the scope of their investigation.

For us to continue our examination of emotions, let us first acknowledge the existence of the obvious parallel between our emotional states and the reflexes taking place in our body. The sight of a favorite food starts the secretion of saliva, but it also is immediately paralleled in our consciousness by a pleasant excitement. The cry of a hunted animal instantly prepares our body for action, but it is also registered in our consciousness as a rising agitation. Our experience indicates that some emotional states, either strong or mild, always accompany our everyday activities.

Emotion emerges as an immediate consequence of an evaluation of a situation from the organism's point of view. Emotions have their origins in the physiological processes, the purpose of which is to prepare the organism for the upcoming effort: an adaptational activity. Physiologists describe emotion as a state in which the reserves of energy stored in the organism are rapidly released during pursuit or defense. It may be said that emotion as experienced in our awareness of ourselves is a trace of an occurring adaptational process, just as the sudden flash of a falling star in the night skies is really the trace of a meteor being burned in the upper layers of the atmosphere.

Stimuli that trigger emotional states can have their sources in the outside environment as well as within the organism itself—stimuli created by illness, for instance.

The distinctive feature of emotion is its qualitative tinge: positive, such as joy or contentment; or negative, such as sorrow or uneasiness. Pleasant emotions accompany the satisfaction of our needs: appeasement of hunger, fulfillment of love, achievement of desired social status, and so on. Unpleasant emotions indicate unfulfilled wants.

Emotion therefore represents in the consciousness a unified physiological and psychological reaction, which from the human point of view might be the best in any given life circumstance. Emotion expresses the value that the situation or object holds for an individual. Pleasure or distress are, then, very sensitive indicators of the degree to which our needs are fulfilled.

Emotions are one of the elementary components of consciousness. We may not like it, but psychological phenomena devoid of some emotional color simply do not exist. Many of us in the industry learned this the hard way. We might have developed a good product that still would not sell. Despite hard facts in our support, negative esthetic emotions generated by the appearance of the product prevented people from buying it.

How can we neutralize such an unfavorable situation? Let us pursue our examination of emotions in search of an answer.

2.5 Emotions of Involuntary Behavior

Continuing our effort to understand the emotional side of human behavior, let us now investigate emotions related to the two previously discussed types of adaptational processes: involuntary (inborn and learned) and rational. We may anticipate that any esthetic emotions related to inborn patterns of behavior will be the strongest and most commonly shared among individuals of the human species.

One of the inborn characteristics of the human species is the manner in which our eye sees and the brain analyzes what the eye registers in the field of vision—the involuntary process of perception. Visual patterns do not have equal value in perception. Chaos and the lack of organization are confusing, while clarity and order facilitate perception. Accordingly, visual chaos tends to generate negative emotions and a clear visual organization pleases the viewer.

The organizing principles of the perception mechanism were investigated by the Gestalt school of psychology. While indifferent to the question of emotion, Gestalt psychologists collected an imposing body of experimental data of great significance to product design. The ability to create esthetic values related to inborn characteristics of perception is one of the most effective tools of the product designer.

We showed earlier that, through conditioning, the stock of involuntary reflexes grows continually with the accumulated experience of an individual. We have also shown that all involuntary adaptational processes function as though mirrored in our consciousness in the form of emotions. Accordingly, a growing experience and accumulation of involuntary responses are paralleled by the enrichment of our emotional responses to changes in the environment.

The continual expansion of emotionally significant stimuli in the life of an individual has been recognized for a very long time. I believe it is reasonable to say that the time-honored term *mental associations* describes the effects of conditioning in the consciousness. Extending this type of reasoning, such an association represents, in the consciousness, the preliminary link of purpose between the unconditioned and conditioned stimuli.

It is because of conditioning that most signals coming to us from the environment have some emotional value to us. According to Pavlov, any outside signal that can be registered by the organism's receptors may serve as a conditioning stimulus.

The enlarging of the stock of stimuli with informative value for the organism leads to the broadening of the emotional sphere of consciousness. Previously indifferent stimuli will gain emotional significance once they have acquired importance. A special color or shape associated with your beloved will always quicken your pulse.

Generation of emotions related to involuntary behavior is spontaneous. In this process there is no recollection of the unconditioned stimuli from which the conditioned stimuli took over the ability of inducing emotions; the memory of the unconditioned stimulus as the original source of the experienced emotion may be totally forgotten. For instance, a person may find an orange circle attractive without recalling the warmth of the orange sun or the taste of the fruit of the orange tree. Conditioned impulses gain autonomy after acquiring the ability to stimulate from unconditioned ones. They will be considered pleasant or repulsive for their own particular qualities alone.

2.6 Emotions of Rational Behavior

When describing the activities of the nervous system, we started with the simple ones: inborn involuntary responses. A step above them are learned involuntary responses. And now we arrive at the level of rational thinking.

Similar to lower nervous activities, rational thinking displays these three already familiar stages: (1) reception of information, (2) analysis, and (3) decision with response. When your car suddenly stops on the highway, you first open the hood in (1) search of information about the trouble. You check the carburetor, battery, electric wires, and fuel lines. You then (2) analyze all the possible causes. Finally, (3) you reach a decision and act appropriately. This is a rational approach to the problem.

This simple example allows us to immediately grasp the difference between lower and higher activities of the nervous system. Automatic responses, inborn or learned, run according to ready patterns. The speed of response is such that we are not aware of any analysis, of any process of comparison and making choices. In rational thinking, however, the selection of a response is preceded by a longer period of time. We are always aware of it. A pause, a preparation of the response, is filled with complex activities of thinking such as comparison, generalization, and deduction.

The most complex activities involve language. We distinguish and identify objects and situations by "thinking with words." Favorable evaluation of the situation produces satisfaction, a positive emotion. Negative assessment is followed by negative emotions. The appearance of emotion is inevitable.

However, the differences between the two types of behavior, involuntary and rational, are as telling as the similarities. We instinctively understand them, but now analysis allows us to grasp these differences with even greater clarity.

In a broad stroke the automatic, involuntary response can be described as *input/output* type of behavior. The "analysis" that separates input from output occurs so rapidly that our broad brush is too crude a tool to depict it.

In the same simplified way, rational response can be described as *input/analysis/output* type of behavior. The major premise of this book is that only the *input/output* type of response is responsible for esthetic emotions.

Thanks to the mechanism of automatic responses, consciousness registers only two sequences of adaptational processes, the first and the last, the stimulus and the final reaction of the organism together with an emotion of attraction or repulsion. How well this pattern describes the little scene in a department store with which I started the book! You see the product that you like (input) and you want to buy it immediately (output). The intermediate sequences of analysis and decision making took place in your subconscious and were fully automatic.

The differences between the types of adaptational assessment/decision processes that have been discussed are further characterized in figure 16. It is readily apparent that its pattern resembles that of figure 15: the appropriate fields correspond to each other. The adaptational processes are represented by the flow of information. The longer the time of decision making, the greater the extent of nervous connections participating in the process.

2.7 Summary on Emotions

The diagrams shown in figures 15 and 16 do not pretend to represent the real structure of psychological phenomena. Rather, they should be treated as a specific, graphic-descriptive summary of the discussion. They are intended to display the complicated life processes in a simplified way. However, nothing is as simple as this in nature. Groups of phenomena, separated for methodological purposes, in reality blend together, merging into one another. Human behavior is characterized by a complex of processes in which reflexive decisions clash with rational ones, thinking with words blends with sequences of sensory-motor analysis, and emotions are moderated by reflection. With these limitations in mind, the intermediate summary of our investigation can be presented as follows.

The primary emotions toward the observed object develop in the process of perception. Their structure is reflexive. In the majority of cases the contact between the object and the viewer ends here, at the level of sensory cognition. At this level, emotion is the only indicator of the object's apparent ability to fulfill the viewer's needs and the autonomy of emotion is undivided in the process of valuation.

An adequately developed mechanism of rational analysis is necessary for a more thorough assessment of perceived values. The prevailing mode of behavior with children and simpletons is emotional. Fully developed minds have the capacity for modifying emotions. Whereas the primary emotional attitude of the viewer toward the object perceived is the result of a purely sensory cognizance, the secondary attitude is its rational modification. Here, the autonomy of emotion is limited in the process of valuation. Emotion shares its autonomy with rational assessment.

As has been shown, the commonly accepted distinction between the processes of emotional and rational valuation does not mean that the latter takes place in a total absence of emotions. This distinction only emphasizes that, in the first case, the experienced emotion is the only criterion of the value recognized in the object. In the second instance, we try to neutralize the emotion during the formation of judgment.

Adaptational activities are characterized by specific dynamics. Within the life processes there is a clear trend of complex forms of behavior evolving into simpler ones. This phenomenon is of course associated with the need for a simplification of the decision-making processes. As much burden as possible is being transferred from the level of rationally derived decisions to the level of involuntary, automatic responses. The latter, we learned, run according to previously conditioned patterns of behavior. Behavior guided by rational thinking and emotions continually gives place to emotions alone.

When emotions displace thinking, knowledge about the environment deteriorates. However, at the same time, the speed at which information is provided rapidly increases. It appears that such a trade-off is favored by evolution.

The dynamics that have been described above are of significant practical consequence. If evolution rewards those forms in which a probing of the environment by the organism takes place primarily through emotions, we must keep in mind the importance of the emotions generated by the world around us as we attempt to reshape it.

2.8 Life Function of Esthetic Emotions

When we began the discussion of emotions, we made the observation that there are no valid reasons for viewing esthetic emotions as structurally different from any other emotions. This, of course, does not mean that all emotions are esthetic. Recall that, although the term has never been defined precisely, the interpretations of esthetic emotion revolve around the same prevailing themes.

First, esthetic emotions are those that start with the senses of seeing and hearing. The scope of this study excludes auditory stimuli from our investigation. Only those emotions generated by visual stimuli remain the object of our continuing interest. Second, the esthetic emotions are those generated by the appearance of the object alone, not by what we have otherwise learned and know about the object. Third, the esthetic judgment is instantaneous; it has the structure of a reflex.

In the diagrams of figures 15, 16, 20, and 25, the esthetic emotions would appear in the spheres of events designated I and II, where the sequences of analysis are so rapid that they are not registered by consciousness. The appreciation of esthetic value is therefore the last link in the chain of transformations to which visual stimuli are subjected in the human psyche. This link expresses the recognition of something as useful, desirable, or purposeful. However, its direct connection with the prior links to the source of this conviction has been broken; it has been submerged in the subconscious.

The esthetic emotions of sphere I are related to inborn patterns of behavior. This type of behavior has been reinforced throughout the span of existence of the human *species*. The process has been long and crude. The balance between the organism and its environment has been reached through the elimination of the less-adapted specimen. The esthetic pleasures of sphere I testify to the existing congruence between visual stimuli and the perceptual capacities of the human species.

The esthetic emotions of sphere II are related to conditioned patterns of behavior and have been formed in the life span of the *individual*. At this level, the balance between human and environment is maintained in the process of trial and error. The desired symbiosis is reached through the application of corrective rewards and punishments. The emotions of esthetic satisfaction or displeasure of sphere II direct an individual toward seeming rewards or warn of apparent punishments.

In conclusion, the sense of visual beauty or ugliness builds on a foundation of purpose. This purpose might never have been consciously experienced, as is typical of natural selection. In the process of conditioning, the purpose is initially recognized, but with time, the described tendency to eliminate superfluity gradually erases awareness of purpose from consciousness. Ultimately, any sense of purposefulness is efficiently eliminated from the esthetic emotion, even though it always looms invisibly in the background.

As noted by the Dutch philosopher Spinoza, "If motion which the nerves receive by means of the eyes from objects before us is conducive to health, those objects are called beautiful; if it is not, those object are called ugly." Today, having the benefit of Maslow's classification of needs, we would call an object beautiful if it is conducive to health, safety, a sense of belonging, esteem, and self-realization.

Thus, the original biological or social function of the human ability to appreciate visual beauty (positive esthetic values), has been to produce a positive emotional attitude toward an object, to testify to its supposed suitability for the viewer. The function of the ability to assess ugliness has been the production of a negative attitude, to repel or to warn.

However, it must be emphasized that, as an indicator of utility, esthetic value provides imprecise evidence. In fact, visual beauty testifies to utility experienced in the past rather than in the present. In other words, esthetic value implies an alleged rather than an actual usefulness of the object to the viewer.

Esthetic value is a poor-quality carrier of information. Its great utility lies in the speed with which it transfers this information—a decisive factor in the majority of life situations.

Chapter 3. Esthetic Values of Industrial Products

3.1 X, Y, and Z Esthetic Values

As has been shown, emotions emerge at all levels of nervous-system activity from the simplest to the most complex responses to environmental stimuli. Our personal experience also suggests that esthetic emotions represent a spectrum of responses rather than a single, homogeneous, identical reaction to various visual stimuli. On one end of this spectrum there are esthetic emotions generated by the sight, for example, of two stripes of color in harmony with each other. At the other extreme are those emotional states generated by the sight, let us say, of a supersonic aircraft or a sports car.

It is also convenient to arrange esthetic values, i.e., visual characteristics responsible for the generation of esthetic emotions, in a similar spectrum. Starting from those of low complexity, universal appeal, and greater suitability for generalization, these values will range to those of growing complexity, increasing subjectivity, and diminishing responsiveness to analysis.

For the purpose of methodology, our discussion on the esthetic values of industrial products will focus on three blocks of values representative of the above spectrum, from the simplest to the most complex.

X values. The first group of esthetic values will be those expressing the order of visual forms, their simplicity and clarity. These values cater to our need to recognize and understand objects. Therefore, we may suggest that, in broader terms, they cater to our need for mental comfort (health) and safety.

Y values. The second group of esthetic values will be those that are conducive to purposefulness and functionality and that communicate the intention for which the products are made. The ability of the product's form to express these values will, it is suggested, gratify the need for successful mental activities or, in broader terms, the need for safety and self-esteem.

Z values. The last group of esthetic values will be derived from fashion, prevailing taste, or the visual culture of the time. It is presumed that these values fulfill the need to belong and for self-esteem and self-realization.

It should not be surprising that the above blocks of esthetic values of industrial products have been arranged in a pattern roughly approximating Maslow's gradation of needs. After all, we have identified esthetic values and the esthetic emotions associated with them as essential elements in the pattern of maintaining a balance between the human organism and its multifaceted environment. Moreover, it has also been shown that the disturbance of this balance is signaled by the emergence of needs.

It can be noticed with respect to the foregoing suggested division of esthetic values that, if those assigned to block X are connected basically with facilitation of perception and are essentially *abstract,* then the values in blocks Y and Z are associated with the *meanings* of the perceived visual forms. This implies a higher level of nervous system activity engaged in the appreciation of values Y and Z.

There is also the implication in the suggested pattern that the values grouped at the X end of the spectrum are akin to emotions related to inborn patterns of behavior, whereas those at the Z end are more conducive to conditioned involuntary responses.

Last, it can be pointed out (without assuming a precision of observation) that from among the classic theories listed in chapter 1, section 1.5, there is an affinity of issues, approaches, and solutions between the "Great Theory" and Gestalt, on the one hand, and those assigned to group X on the other. Similar kinships exist between the Functionalist theory and group Y and between Associational Esthetics and group Z.

The following sections of the book will be devoted to further investigation of the esthetic values in groups X, Y, and Z.

3.2 Block X - Visual Order as Esthetic Value

In a review of the literature of the psychology of perception it would be difficult to find a more comprehensive theory devoted to this subject than that developed by Gestalt psychology.

Gestalt psychology has been concerned solely with the mechanism of perception and not at all with the value of visual patterns as perceived by the viewer. Nevertheless, the findings of the gestaltists have long been applied in teaching the composition of successful, i.e., widely accepted visual designs. Today, there is hardly an author on this subject who would find it possible to approach visual design without frequent reference to the psychology of Gestalt.

The gestaltists have shown that the process of perception does not necessarily occur in the form of a joining together of the smaller components within the field of vision, but takes place instantaneously through perception of larger unitary wholes. Gestalt psychologists have collected a rich documentation of perception mechanisms—the tendencies of the mind to interpret real, observed systems in a special, orderly, organized, and simplified way.

The classic experiments confirming these tendencies were based on brief presentations of various patterns to the subjects of the test. The test subjects were requested to reconstruct the patterns as accurately as possible. The experiments demonstrated the tendency of the subjects to simplify the patterns in a manner that indicated the existence of regularities. Figure 29 illustrates the results of a typical experiment.

In another experiment, test subjects were confronted with graphic patterns, derivatives of the simplest, most regular geometrical figures. The deviations of the patterns from their archetypes consisted of slight deformations. The subjects were then asked to form their opinions about the deficiencies of the pictures. The corrections that test subjects made consistently restored the regularity of the archetypes (fig. 30).

These and similar experiments demonstrated the existence of an active disposition in the process of perception toward organizing the multitude of elements in the field of vision into certain unitary wholes according to patterns encoded in the nervous system. Any collection of visual stimuli is simplified in the process of perception to the degree that is possible in a given set of circumstances.

What does tendency to simplify mean? What are the dynamics of this type of activity of the nervous system? In the most obvious of its meanings, the term *simplicity* is the opposite of the term *complexity* in the sense that a *unit* is the opposite of a *multitude*. In this manner of understanding it, the simplicity of the system is associated with the small number of its components. It could be referred to as an *absolute simplicity*.

The simplicity of a visual pattern can also be *relative*. In that case, it applies to the structure of relationships among the components of the system. Consequently, a square will commonly be considered to be simpler than the triangle contrasted to it (as for instance in figure 31), even though the square is composed of a greater number of components. The edges of the square are of equal length and are equally spaced from the center. The lines that form the square lie in two directions, vertical and horizontal, and all the angles of the figure are equal. The pattern is characterized by a considerable degree of symmetry along four axes. In contrast, the triangle is constructed of a lesser number of elements, but they differ from one another in length and position; its construction shows no symmetry. It appears that both absolute and relative simplicity greatly facilitate the process of perception.

3.3 Synthesizing Tendencies of Perception

Gestalt psychologists point out several tendencies of perception, which, when followed in design, result in visual patterns of enhanced simplicity (fig. 32).

The Tendency to Rhythmic Forms. *Rhythm* is commonly understood as the repetition of visual elements of similar shape, position in space, color, and so on (fig. 33). Besides rigid mechanical rhythms such as that of a threaded bolt, there exist subtle and lively rhythms typical of nature. Flowers in a meadow, despite differences in shape, size, and color, endow the field with unquestionably rhythmic character (fig. 34). When the discipline of the rhythm further softens, the visual pattern acquires what is called homogeneity.

The Tendency to Homogeneous Forms. *Homogeneity,* closely related to rhythm, is the standardization of the means of expression. Homogeneity in a square is a result of standardizing the straight sections making up its edges and angles (fig. 35). The redesigned lathe in figure 37 has considerable visual homogeneity because the concept of a rectangle was applied in shaping the major elements of its form, and the shapes of its control levers are closely related. The standardization of radii in applied curvatures and the standardization of bolt and screw sizes, labels, control indicators, and steering elements are conducive to the increased homogeneity of industrial forms.

The Tendency to Symmetrical Forms. *Symmetry* is that peculiarity of form whereby, after some changes of position, the new positions are identical in appearance to the original one (fig. 38). In forms of this type, a visual rhythm is produced as an effect of the characteristic mirror image of the elements of form on both sides of a center point, axis, or plane of symmetry. Symmetrical systems provide an example of a special type of rhythm. They have a rich tradition in the history of visual design, and symmetry is even insisted upon by some as a mandatory condition of the esthetic quality of form.

The Tendency to Continuity of Direction. *Continuity of direction* seems to have a stronger appeal than symmetry. In figure 39, symmetrical patterns A and B lose their autonomy to larger, asymmetrical forms but display greater continuity of contour patterns as soon as they are brought into direct contact with each other (fig. 39C). It is worth noting that the new, stronger patterns (39D and E) are also more *compact* than A and B in the sense described earlier (fig. 50).

The Tendency to Geometrize manifests itself by favoring those forms that have distinctive geometrical traits, i.e., those built from straight lines, circles, ellipses, and so on. In this regard, the preference for the vertical and horizontal is characteristic. One of the unquestionable factors explaining this phenomenon is the action of the gravitational field, which enforces the natural formation of masses. The surface of a calm lake is horizontal; that of a freely hanging plumb line is vertical. Consequently, our accommodation to these two main directions frequently has a practical meaning, especially in design and construction. However, the need to seek and favor the geometrical vertical and horizontal that irresistibly imposes itself goes beyond the practical reasons for their application.

The principle of the easy perception of geometrical shapes is used by some designers almost directly (fig. 40), especially when the chosen methods of manufacturing support it (fig. 41). In other cases, the principle is applied more to the general outline of the form than to its final configuration (fig. 43).

The Tendency to a Limited Number of Elements is the response of the brain to a special "discomfort." If the number of visual stimuli exceeds the perceptive capabilities of the nervous system, the emotional reaction of the observer is negative; and his mind immediately tries to simplify the visual patterns. We can perceive only a limited number of elements at a time, and when there are more than five or six elements, the mind joins individual components into larger wholes. Systemizing the chaos of stars into constellations for better understanding is an indication of this tendency. Purposeful shaping of a form in such a way as to avoid too many conspicuous components adds to its value in terms of generating positive emotional attitude.

The twelve chaotically distributed dots in figure 44 will make a pattern that is more easily perceived if they are grouped into two sets of six dots each. For the same reason, the control board in figure 36A is usually preferred over the one in figure 36B.

Of course, the postulate of a limited number of elements cannot always be realized literally because there are constraints of function, design, or fabrication. However, these constraints frequently can be modified without detrimental effects on the operational characteristics of the product and will result in an improvement in the appearance of that product's form.

It is impossible in the design of a typewriter, for instance, to limit the number of elements by reducing the number of keys. However, the principle has been followed by emphasizing the unity of the typewriter's body, by covering the previously exposed mechanism, and by the visual standardization of the keyboard (fig. 45). Similarly, the evolution of the front of the automobile shows the tendency toward a reduction of the number of visually significant elements without detriment to function (figs. 46 and 47).

The Tendency to Compact Forms manifests itself in the preference for closed forms, which have a tight arrangement of elements, decisively separating from the environment the space they enclose or fill, such as a ball or a cube (fig. 49). Such forms are clearly organized and unequivocally understood. In contrast to such organization are open forms with vaguely defined borders and loosely connected elements, which can be interpreted ambiguously, such as the crown of a leafless tree or a three-dimensional truss structure.

Compactness or cohesiveness is perhaps best described as the ratio of the surface of the given form to its volume or, in flat forms, as the ratio of the length of the contour to the surface. When several forms are compared, the most compact will be the one for which the value of this ratio is lowest (fig. 50). Of two patterns made from the same components, pattern B (fig. 48) is the more compact.

The history of the development of industrial forms reflects the influence of the tendency to compact forms. Even though this development has been partly the result of technological factors, the evolution from loose to compact forms is undeniable. It can be traced, for instance, in the maturation of the forms of automobiles, typing machines, sewing machines, and gas heaters (figs. 52, 53, 54).

The Tendency to Visual Organization on a Grid of Straight Lines is, perhaps, one of the manifestations of the tendency to geometrize. It manifests itself as the spontaneous tendency to search for straight lines in the field of vision and to arrange visual patterns on a grid of straight lines.

This postulate, derived from the way our mechanism of perception works, can be followed literally in design (fig. 56D). However, it is sometimes applied only to the general outline of the form, and then even to organic, streamlined forms, that are quite remote from rigid geometrical structures (fig. 56C).

The use of straight lines to bind together the elements of design can be found in the oldest known artifacts and samples of architecture (see figs. 56A and B). This indicates that the unifying tendency of straight lines running across design patterns was instinctively grasped and used long before the experiments of Gestalt psychology. This is also true with respect to other simplifying tendencies of perception investigated by Gestalt psychologists.

In visual communication, geometric and compact forms are as useful as those opposed to them. The specific objective of an artist painting a picture can dictate the application of loosely organized forms rather than those displaying compactness, rhythm, and homogeneity. A product designer may face a situation in which the product function makes it impossible to increase the cohesiveness of its form. Bicycles and sailboats are good examples of such products. However, in general the utilitarian objectives of industrial products are well served by the application of organizing principles discovered by Gestalt psychology.

3.4 Block Y: Functionalism as Esthetic Value

Visual tidiness or neatness is among the oldest and most widely accepted components of esthetic value. The esthetic appreciation of function, fitness, utility, or purpose yields only to that of visual order in its widespread appeal.

Functional forms, the most ideal examples of which are found in nature, are always the result of the balance between their environment and the resistance the forms offer (fig. 91). In this process, it is a law of the economy of evolution that natural forms seek the lines that require the least energy and material to survive. Its hydrodynamic shape allows a fish to thrust forward with a minimal effort. Animal bones, with their round cross-section, hard crust, and light, porous filling, provide another example of this economy.

Good design follows the laws governing natural organisms. It is not an accident that the term *organic design* has become synonymous with *functional design*. In the balance between external and internal forces, functional design is an extension of the work of nature.

The appreciation of visually communicated fitness of form as a positive esthetic value has its roots in the previously described process of the conditioning of emotional responses. This conditioning occurs within the feedback relationship between subject and environment every time visual stimuli are assessed to indicate situations beneficial to the subject. The reasoning behind a stimulation dies away with time because of the desired efficiency of responses. From that time on, the human, without observing the actual practicality of an object, reacts positively to visual patterns that communicate the purposefulness of that object. Thus, the visual communicativeness of a product's utility is the carrier of esthetic value. Its increase leads to an increase of visual beauty.

3.5 Universal Appeal of Functionality

The functionally conditioned esthetic values (Y) lie between those derived from the mechanism of perception (X) and those of cultural origins (Z). Functional esthetic values are less universal than those of X which represent visual clarity and order. At the same time, the esthetic appreciation of functionality is more widely shared than that of the diverse and transient, culturally derived esthetic values Z.

Nonetheless, the appeal of functionally conditioned esthetic values is widespread and well established, partially because the performance of machines and the development of their forms are governed by absolute laws of nature. Even people who are not directly involved in matters of technology can understand the principles of the basic laws of mechanics. Purposefulness of form, i.e., its appropriateness to the function performed, can be perceived even by the nonprofessional provided these qualities are clearly conveyed through the visual arrangement of the design elements.

The origins of the human ability to perceive purposefulness have their roots in the execution of everyday life functions. One's own body is the best instrument for learning the laws of nature and the functioning of simple mechanisms formed in agreement with these laws. For instance:

— A person standing with legs positioned far apart has increased stability, (Read: wider base stabilizes the mass, fig. 61).

— The silhouette of a luggage porter with heavily loaded arms displays shortening and broadening. (Read: the dimensions of material undergo a reduction under a compressing force and an increase in the plane perpendicular to the direction of the force).

— Extending an arm while holding a weight increases the bending moment acting upon the arm. The moment must be compensated for by an increased tension of muscles in the shoulder. (Read: a larger force applied to a cantilever beam requires the increase of a fixation moment, figs. 59 and 60).

These and similar experiences and their repeated occurrence will cause some visual patterns to be inevitably associated with specific functions, situations, and activities. Symmetrical patterns with a broad base will suggest inertness. Asymmetry, or patterns showing a tendency toward visual separation from the base, will provide a sense of mobility. Overcoming the resistance of such media as water and air is associated with streamlined shapes. When the resistance of the medium increases (e.g., wood and metal), streamlined shapes give way to sharp forms, such as those of the nail, knife, or cutting tool, which more effectively overcome the greater density of material.

It is no accident that there are so many machine components named for parts of the human body (e.g., arm, foot, and head).

The ways in which children less than two or three years old play with toys show their lack of concern with the forces of gravity and indicate that they have not yet mastered "practical statics." At a later age they are capable of an almost flawless application of the laws of mechanical balance, even though theoretical formulas are not known to them.

3.6 Visual Symbolism of Function

We have assumed for our purpose that mental associations represent in consciousness reflexes conditioned in the process of everyday activities. Some of the most universal associations are those conditioned in performing common and simple tasks and connected with perception of movement, gravity, balance, distribution of forces, and so on. The visual patterns that trigger these associations—formal schemes corresponding to various states of balance of masses and forces—enlarge the supply of means available to the product designer for the expression of product function.

Even though the organization of associations in the process of design can be accomplished by reverting to a visual pattern of a concrete, specific object, in the majority of cases this process depends on achieving the desired expression (or informativeness of form) with the help of a means of expression typical of a *class* of objects of a similar function. An example borrowed from graphic arts (fig. 65) illustrates the point. A flattened letter *V* and its inverted image make a pair of opposed symbols expressing joy and sadness or, in engineering terms, an outburst of energy or mobility on one side and exhaustion of energy or inertness on the other. The graphic representations of concrete objects placed below these symbols suggest the origins of emotional climates associated with them.

Visual patterns that allow expression of the functional characteristics of industrial forms are, of course, essential in product design. Let us examine, for example, the function of movement.

An object moving on the surface of the water leaves behind a trail in the shape of a wedge. The contours of a fish, arrow, knife, bird, automobile, the mobility of which is an essential characteristic of their function, are made of a cluster of converging lines (fig. 63). Slanting contour lines, meeting in a leading point of movement, are dictated by the nature of the penetration by these objects into a material medium—penetration that overcomes the cohesion of such a medium.

One may point out another source of the dynamism sensed in the described visual patterns. Slanted objects suggest real or potential movement by their contrast with positions that imply resting: vertical hanging or lying on a horizontal surface. As a result of this type of regularity, crossing slanted lines will always trigger associations with the function of movement.

Figure 66 contrasts, among other things, the dynamism of slanted lines with the static pattern of a grid constructed of horizontal and vertical lines. Other pairs of graphic symbols contrast a static symmetry, inert broad base, and "uncommitted" scattered particles with the dynamism of asymmetry, undercut base, and particles organized along a line that suggests movement.

The changes shown in figure 67, directed toward making the silhouette of the automobile more dynamic, were made by application of the above observations. The symmetry of the visual pattern has been disrupted; front and rear undercutting of the car body base has weakened the sense of immobility; horizontal elongation has emphasized the direction of movement; and horizontals and verticals have given place to slanted lines.

Another task frequently facing the designer is the visual communication of gravitational stability, the mechanical balance of a system.

Why do we prefer forms to be solidly located in space? Most likely because stable objects around us gratify our need for safety. In any event, as indicated earlier, visual patterns project a sense of stability through associations with commonly recognized laws of physical balance. We have investigated the relationship between the perception of movement or inertia and the horizontal versus vertical characteristics of the lines describing the form. The other associations are drawn from an intuitive understanding of the principle of scale: a mass placed some distance from the point of equilibrium is balanced by a mass twice as heavy at half the distance on the other side of the equilibrium point.

In visual terms, "weight" is proportional to the size of the form, and black forms are "heavier" than white (fig. 68). Shiny surfaces convey a sense of lightness when compared to flat ones. Overall, as with any exercise, the time spent on design contributes greatly to an understanding of the subtle relationship between perceptual and physical balance in the form.

3.7 Form and Function

Those who are reluctant to accept a purely esthetic intervention in product design usually refer to Sullivan's phrase "form follows function." They believe that the faithful following of this precept will automatically result in the achievement of an attractive form. The practice of design does not confirm this expectation. To borrow an example from civil engineering, there are few objects whose function is more precisely defined in technical terms than the bridge. Theoretically, then, all bridges built to the same specification should look pretty much the same. However, the tremendous variety of existing designs, in visual terms from average to breathtaking, testifies to the existence of a considerable margin for esthetic intervention in purely technical projects. Figures 37, 51, and 113 give examples that show that it is possible to greatly improve the appearance of products without changing their major characteristics.

The analysis of forms of acclaimed esthetic quality leads to the conviction that, in part at least, such forms generate positive reactions because they display what might be called an "excess" of functionality, i.e., some surplus value in their purposefulness. It might be said that the functionality of the product acquires a decidedly esthetic quality if it is allowed slight redundance. This small excess of functionality makes the function visible or more clearly visible and is intended to catch the attention of the observer and gain decorative autonomy.

A frequently cited example of "excess" functionality is provided by the shapes of columns in the temples of ancient Greece. Their outline displays a slight convexity, which emphasizes the work of compression forces acting upon the columns.

A similar interpretation can be applied to the solution chosen in the design of a mixer (fig. 71). The work of its cantilever beam has been emphasized by the simulation of increasing cross section growth toward the point of fixation when in fact its upper and bottom faces are parallel—in response, no doubt, to production or other design requirements.

The desired "excess" of functionality is modified by the requirement for simplicity. The merit of simplicity was stressed in the discussion of X esthetic values and it is equally important at the level of Y esthetic values. We are not satisfied to let form follow function in just any way. In product design we strive for economy, efficiency, clarity, and simplicity in both technical and esthetic solutions.

Good designers instinctively apply what in the philosophy of science is known as "Ockham's razor." William Ockham, a medieval English philosopher, formulated this famous principle of economy in formal logic. In essence, the principle dictates a ruthless elimination of all elements of a system that are not necessary to justify the system's existence. No solution should be considered final if a simpler one can be found.

The necessity of applying a curvature to the Greek column was a purely esthetic one. The tension between the desired simplicity and the "excess" of functionality is one of the driving forces in the creative process of design. A successful reconciliation of these two values is one of the recognized measures of a designer's talent.

3.8 Block Z: Responsiveness to the Prevailing Visual Taste

Moving from simpler to more complex esthetic reactions, we finally arrive at the level of cultural and social factors. The controversial issues of style, fashion, or current vogue belong to this group.

We understand the world around us in a different way than did our ancestors in the nineteenth century or in the Middle Ages. Our means of expression, mental associations, and conditioned reflexes are different today from what they were in the past. They undergo continual change, and we change our visual world accordingly. The changes in our understanding are reflected in our architecture, product design, sculpture, graphics, and painting.

Product designers, whether they are aware of it or not, will always be influenced by contemporary culture. Product users living in the climate of a given visual culture will, also unconsciously, more easily accept those forms for which they are the best prepared.

The State of Technology. The visual culture of the time is a result, to a considerable degree, of the state of available technology. The Egyptian Pyramids, impressive as they are, rely on the simplest possible concept: piling up stones and enlarging the cross section of the structure proportionally to the growing weight. Romanesque and Gothic architects discovered the load-carrying capabilities of the arch, which vastly increased the horizons of human creativity. The introduction of steel into architecture gave us shell structures that can cover an entire athletic field in one span and gave us buildings that at some point will, no doubt, reach the height of one mile. The concept of such a towering structure was proposed by Frank Lloyd Wright.

In fact, it may be said that the efficient application of available technologies will surely lead to forms that reflect the visual culture of the times. Let us consider, for instance, the exactness and repetitiveness of today's manufacturing processes. They result in the production of forms conveying a sense of reliability, dependability, solidity—in a word, good quality. It did not take long before the precision of contemporary industrial forms came to be recognized as the esthetic value of those forms.

Centers of Power. Next to the influence of technology on prevailing visual taste is the influence of people in positions of power and wealth. In the past, without exception, visual tastes were shaped by two major centers of power: the leaders of ruling classes and the churches. Today, as the power base of all political and social movements broadens, the centers that dictate contemporary styles and fashions are multiplied.

Stimuli Unrelated to the Objects' Function. The sources of specific esthetic attitudes, idiosyncrasies, and tastes are many and are highly diverse. An object can be considered attractive irrespective of its purpose; its visual pattern may trigger conditioned emotional responses originating in previous experiences unrelated to the function of the product. For instance, streamlined shapes can be captivating because they symbolize speed and ease of movement or situations of sexual intimacy, with little or no actual relationship to the functional effectiveness of the object.

In such cases, we talk about some activities or situations, which initially served only practical purposes, being transformed into autonomically pleasant or unpleasant experiences. People used to hunt for food; today they do it for fun. A sports sedan is not designed for racing, but its "fast" body lifts the spirits of its owner. The mechanism of this phenomenon of transferring values was discussed in some detail in chapter 2.

In this respect, Skinner's experiments dealing with the "superstitions" of pigeons, i.e., irrationalities in their behavior, were very revealing. A number of pigeons were placed on a restricted diet until they reached 75 percent of their normal weight. Then they were fed quantities of food at equal time intervals. It was found that, with great predictability, pigeons continued the specific body movements that they had happened to be performing at the first appearance of food. Their random behavior was fixed and reinforced as a reflex conditioned by the reward of food. One of the pigeons performed a dance of rotation, another developed an involuntary movement of raising an invisible obstacle with its head, all to "conjure" more food. Without making a direct comparison between this behavior and the superstitions of humans, we can point out that the analogy is striking.

This pattern of conditioning may explain why those who cannot accomplish what is desirable nor achieve what is attractive to them receive at least partial satisfaction through activities and objects associated with those things and people they consider attractive. Popular parroting of the behavior, clothing, and manners of celebrities undoubtedly reflects this type of conditioning. Teenagers who wear clothing resembling that of their idols seem to share their idols' success. The plastic imitation of oak veneer in contemporary automobiles simulates the interiors of early twentieth-century carriages of noblemen. The owner of such an automobile becomes "noble" by associating himself with visual symbols of the former ruling class.

Affinity with Technological Leaders. In the field of industrial products there is a clear propensity for imitating the visual patterns associated with the "leader" in a technology. The success of aeronautics brought a flurry of aerodynamic shapes in the thirties and forties. The breaking of the sound barrier and the subsequent sharpening of aircraft silhouettes resulted in the phenomenon of well-defined, clear-cut shapes for many products. The success of electronic calculating machines influences the appearance of many industrial and consumer goods, which come to resemble computers irrespective of their actual function.

Overcoming Boredom. The tendencies that have been described are reinforced by the human need and search for newness. The search for new, visually fresh products is partially satisfied by the progress of technology. But even the fantastic progress that we are witnessing today seems not to be on a par with our insatiable desire for eliminating the slightest trace of boredom. Our ambition or vanity to be among those who promote and lead, who constitute the cream of society, the best, or at least to resemble them, undoubtedly also influences the trend toward the new. Newly reshaped, repackaged products are welcomed every day with almost guaranteed market success.

To remind myself of the infinite opportunities for untried design solutions, I like to recall Frank Lloyd Wright's Fallingwater weekend house. The pylons of the foundation were driven into the bed of a rocky waterfall. The concrete blocks of the house were then literally built around the cascades of water, thus creating the illusion of a mass of water rushing through the living quarters of the house. The originality of approach and the element of surprise provide the desired spark of excitement when one sees the design.

3.9 Transitions of Culture

X esthetic values are as stable as their biological foundations. They evolve with the slowness of corrections occurring in the biological make-up of the human species. In fact, we do not record any meaningful changes in the structure of X values since the time of the oldest preserved artifacts.

The situation could not be more different when considering the plasticity of Z values. At this level, esthetic preferences are not only changeable but they may change several times within a single generation.

Technical revolutions can change the perception of the state of technology within five to ten years. This certainly happened when plastics were introduced. Social revolutions impose a change of role models in an even shorter time. Yesterday it was a self-made man raising himself from the poverty of a shoeshine boy to the status of a millionaire. Today it may be a young radical throwing his life away over a dream of revolution. Even seemingly constant characteristics of human responses, such as a favorable reaction toward symbols of sexual significance, change their value and intensity depending on the momentary bent of the society toward promiscuity or restraint.

All these and other transitory colorations of a culture are instantaneously amplified by the human tendency to imitate others. This herd instinct, probably the manifestation of the need for safety and a sense of belonging, has never been better illustrated than in the amusing and at the same time frightening anecdote once told by financier Bernard Baruch:

> "Have you ever seen, in some wood, on a sunny quiet day, a cloud of flying midges—thousands of them—hovering, apparently motionless, in a sunbeam?...Yes?...Well, did you ever see the whole flight, each mite apparently preserving its distance from all others, suddenly move, say three feet, to one side or the other? Well, what made them do that? A breeze? I said a quiet day. But try to recall—did you ever see them move directly back again in the same unison? Well, what made them do that? Great human mass movements are slower of inception but much more effective."

Truly, a product designer who is trying to emulate or influence fashion can hardly be offered more meaningful advice.

T. S. Eliot's reflection on cultivating the discipline of esthetics comes to mind at this point: "There is no method except to be very intelligent." But even this seems to be too optimistic an assessment of our predicament. Practice demonstrates that what we call a "design hit" appears very rarely and always as a result of instinct rather than intelligence. This instinct reveals itself in a superb design talent and is really effective in combination with a healthy addition of pure luck. This conclusion should not discourage us. After all, the fashionable "hits" represent only a small percentage of products. The vast majority of successful products result from clear visual organization and a good sense of functionality.

3.10 Esthetic Mediation in the Design Process

A product design process in which esthetic objectives are one of the goals eludes attempts at easy characterization. Creative pursuit governs itself with its own laws, of which the most prominent is the one requiring no restraining formulas in the approach to a design problem. Therefore, it is not unusual that the work may start not with a definition of the function of the product and its technical characteristics but with an urgent esthetic vision that nags at the designer's creative sensibilities until it is brought to reality.

However, in the overwhelming majority of cases the process of product design begins with the specification of their technical and operational requirements. What happens next is a creative reconciliation of conflicts between the technical and esthetic directives of the designed product.

The technically and esthetically conscious product designer will try to reconcile any conflict by cautiously gravitating towards esthetic solutions without disturbing the product's technical rationality. For instance, if the technically correct arrangement (A) of figure 76 can be modified (B) without detriment to its function, such a solution would be judged preferable.

On the other hand, stipulations of visual functionality may require measures to the contrary. Suppose the smoothly blended squares of figure 77C fulfill the requirements of a technical directive. In addition, the clarity of its organization is beyond immediate criticism. However, we may still notice a mild esthetic inadequacy in the form since the second square from the right plays a special functional role but its functional uniqueness is not communicated. In such a case a modification (fig. 77D) might improve the esthetic appropriateness of the form.

In conclusion, esthetic mediation in the design process may run as follows:

First, the components of the product are laid down in an arrangement that best fits its inner interrelationships as well as outside functions. Then, questions are allowed to surface. Can the original arrangement be modified without injury to other characteristics of the product and in a way that responds to human preferences for symmetry, visual cohesiveness, closeness, and so on? Can the parts be reshaped to obtain the effect of homogeneity and rhythm? How can the function of the product best be described and then translated into nonverbal visual equivalents? Can a current fashion be suggested in the product's form? Shall it have streamlined, organic shapes or crisp, clearly defined forms? Cool or warm colors?

The work proceeds with attention alternately shifting from technical to esthetic and back to technical objectives. Minor adjustments in one area are followed by major adjustments in the other. Over time, the designer develops a sense of the desired unity. Not infrequently, the results will surprise even the designer. By responding to the functional requirements the designer also aims, even without trying, at the esthetic objectives. But a change intended purely for the refinement of appearance may bring with it an unexpected technical improvement. This, of course, is nothing other than the manifestation of the phenomenon of esthetic value growing on the foundation of purpose.

For instance, moving several times through the process of designing cantilever beams will teach a designer that for the efficient use of material, the cross section of the beam should grow toward the fixation. In time, the designer will automatically draw cantilever beams of that shape, finding them more attractive. Frequent application of rationally derived solutions have gradually implanted the technically correct responses in the designer's subconscious. They emerge then from the subconscious in the guise of esthetically motivated responses. How many times have we heard experienced designers say: "This must be good since it looks good."

It was emphasized earlier that esthetic value may provide imperfect, deceptive evidence about the utility of a product. This fact gives a basis for two approaches.

One approach introduces the meaning of "honesty" in design. This concept rejects categorically any of the camouflaging purposes of esthetic values.

Within this concept, a plastic veneer with a wood-grain pattern is "dishonest" and therefore unacceptable.

The other approach considers the disguising capabilities of esthetic values an important resource in product development. Within this concept, an esthetic deception may be acceptable or even desirable. If a wood-grain pattern printed on vinyl makes people happy and if it sells, let it be. After all, disguising the product may also be functional. This is the case, for instance, when visual chaos is muted by the addition of a cover or a shielding panel.

The choice of approach in design, that of "honesty" or the other possibility—let's call it "pragmatism"—depends on the temperament of a designer, the marketing philosophy of a manufacturer, the market segment to be satisfied, the nature of the product, and current fashion. Which of the two approaches is "better" I will not judge, provided the pursuit of esthetic goals does not compromise the product's utility. The bottom line is that it is more a matter of results than morality; if we forget about it, a brief preliminary success will soon be followed by a recognition of inferior quality and a frequently fatal reduction in sales.

A good product designer will strive for the optimum balance among the characteristics of the product. This does not apply only to the user's assessment of the product's quality. The modification of the tractor in figure 114 brought not only an improvement in the product's appearance but also sizable direct gains to its manufacturer. The number of body parts was reduced from twenty-nine to fifteen and the cost of components was cut by $100,000 per annum, 20 percent of the original cost.

Once tried, an integrated process of design, which combines technical thinking with esthetic approach, becomes as fascinating as any creative process. What might have begun with superficial changes that brought some elements of visual order to the form slowly acquires exciting complexity. The design process becomes more aggressive, the goals more challenging, and the tastes more discriminating. At this level the real selection begins. It becomes clear which of us should pursue a different career and who displays a distinct talent for design.

3.11 Summary

More frequently than not, the first impulse of purchasing is related to the appearance of the product. What can be done to the visual quality of the product to motivate the purchaser?

The approach pursued in this book is that of an engineer solving a problem not yet fully explained by science. In such a situation, simplifications and shortcuts are justified by success in finding an acceptable practical solution.

Usually, motivation can be accomplished by promising to fulfill somebody's needs. Human needs range from body needs to spiritual needs, from the need for nourishment to those of prestige and self-esteem.

The indicators of a degree of fulfillment of needs are emotions. If our needs are fulfilled, we are happy, and the absence of something needed makes us upset.

Esthetic emotions emerge immediately at the sight of an object. This immediacy makes the arrival of esthetic emotions resemble a reflex. Pursuing this analogy, we have divided esthetic emotions into two groups: those related to inborn behavior and those related to acquired involuntary behavior.

At the first level, positive esthetic emotions toward the object perceived testify to an agreement between the observed visual patterns and the way our brain analyzes what the eye sees. Order and clarity generate positive esthetic emotions, while chaos and ambiguity arouse negative esthetic emotions. For the purpose of methodology, order and clarity have been named *X esthetic values*.

At the level of learned involuntary behavior, positive esthetic emotions indicate that the observed visual patterns are associated with things and situations considered good to the onlooker on the basis of previous conditioning. There are two groups of this type of conditioning.

One group is made up of things and situations common to all people and associated with the basic life functions such as eating, walking, sleeping, working, and resting. Esthetic values at this level are in visual patterns that express the purposefulness of objects in supporting these basic life functions. They are esthetic values of functionality and have been named *Y esthetic values*.

Finally, there are *Z esthetic values*, those of fashion, current style, or vogue. In broad terms, Z values relate to the place of the onlooker in society, to the need to share experiences with larger groups, to feelings of importance.

It is hoped that a simplified interpretation of the esthetic values of industrial products will help designers develop products of a broader market acceptance. Designers can do so by applying the principles of visual order (esthetic value X), clearly communicated function (Y), and reference proceeding from the visual culture of the time (Z).

The designer who recognizes and accepts both technological and esthetic values expands the spectrum of design choices. In a world governed by technology, esthetic factors represent both the dissent against rigid rationality and the search for the ideal.

Part

3

Commentaries and Bibliography

Commentaries

(The headlines of the commentaries refer to the titles of the chapters and sections of the book.)

Introduction

I.1   Has This Ever Happened to You?

I.1.1   Which industrial products are the objects of our investigation? The products of particular interest to us in this study are those that meet the following criteria:

(1) Products manufactured by mass production using modern fabrication methods; (2) products in which engineering plays an essential role in the design and development process; (3) products whose design and function are relatively complex; (4) products whose interaction with the user is fundamental to function; (5) products characterized by a relatively long period of service.

It immediately becomes evident that the above outline leaves outside the scope of our investigation such industries as the glass, ceramics, fabric, clothing, and shoe industries. Clearly within the focus of our attention are the automotive, machine, aircraft, electric, and electronic industries and their products, as follows: (1) Automotive products, highway and off-highway; (2) aircraft and spacecraft; (3) marine industry products; (4) other transportation equipment such as rail and rope vehicles and magnetic levitation trains; (5) production and construction machines and tools; (6) home and office appliances.

The above objects share not only the previously described characteristics of complex industrial products but also the basic materials from which those products are made, mainly metals and plastics, as well as the production methods used.

I.1.2 What elements of the discipline of esthetics will be the focus of our attention? Historically, the development of esthetics has gone in two directions: (1) Esthetics has either been considered a knowledge of beauty and of psychological phenomena associated with the perception of beauty, or (2) it has been considered a general theory of art.

As the theory of art, esthetics:

— describes how objects of art were created in the past,

— prescribes how those who create objects of art are to work, how they are to use their tools and materials,

— explains why the objects of art acquire their quality, and what determines their impact and excellence.

This book is not about art but is solely concerned with the first of alternative paths of esthetics: the issues of visual beauty—specifically the issues of visual beauty as applied to the design and development of industrial products.

I.2   The Method

I.2.1   Can product esthetics be pursued as a separate subject?.

The transition from handmade, individually crafted products to the wide application of industrial methods and mass production has seen convulsions of great proportions.

The first mass-produced industrial products of the nineteenth century generated strong disapproval in the more sensitive segment of the market. Unfortunately, the initial reaction to criticism was the emergence of a superficial "beautification" of the products. Cast-iron roses added to the base of a sewing machine were far from the most extreme example of this type of approach.

The twentieth century produced a swing in a radically different direction. "Form follows function" became the order of the day. Unfortunately, this concept, when followed religiously, too frequently led to the creation of gray, spiritless products lacking individuality. While not totally rejected or forgotten, product esthetics has become a slightly embarrassing issue and has certainly lost its autonomy. When discussed in a circle of specialists, it has appeared at best as a by-product of design activities. The cast-iron rose has seemed to brand the sensitivities of the design community with a feeling of shame.

Today we are entering a phase of deserved maturity. We understand that as all the components and functions of the human organism support each other in sustaining life, so it is to the benefit of the designed product that we approach its characteristics in an integrated fashion. The utility of the product will suffer if a structural engineer searches for an optimum design without considering function. The cost of maintenance may be rendered prohibitive if expenditures on production are the only consideration. Manufacturing cost can make a product uncompetitive if its appearance has been improved by added material and processes rather than by developing the natural esthetic values that are hidden in the product's form.

At the same time, we have reached a level of self-confidence; we can look at problems of product esthetics in the way we separately study materials science, the strength of materials, or the organization of production. None of these fields can be explored optimally without considering the others. But we can learn the most about each different field only when, without removing the subject of our investigation from the integral whole, we place a spotlight on it in its natural setting and within its inherent interrelationships.

I.2.2 What sources have we drawn from? The theoretical aspects of attraction one feels toward objects of visual quality were, historically, a subject of the investigations of philosophy, psychology, and the practitioners of design.

In philosophy, the subject was investigated in particular by the German school, including such prominent representatives as Baumgarten and Kant. In our times, some of the important names in philosophical discourse on esthetic values are Read, Arnheim, and Tatarkiewicz.

In psychology and physiology, the sources of special value to our investigation are those associated with Pavlov, Wertheimer, and Maslow. The theoretical aspects of visual forms in design were analyzed by Sullivan, Le Corbusier, Gropius, and others.

The commentaries that follow (I.2.3–I.2.13) provide information about some of the people whose work and thought influenced my investigation. The bibliography includes some of their works, carried forward in this book.

I.2.3 Alexander Gottlieb Baumgarten (1714–1762), a German philosopher, introduced the term *(a)esthetics* and defined the experience of beauty as the sensory recognition of perfection.

I.2.4 Immanuel Kant (1724–1804), a German philosopher, taught that esthetic judgment is not connected with the practical value of the object being considered and that it applies not to the whole object but to its form only.

I.2.5 Sir Herbert Read (1893–1968), an English theoretician of art, wrote the pioneering work on the esthetics of industrial products, *Art and Industry*.

I.2.6 Rudolf Arnheim (1904–), was born in Germany and has lived in the United States since 1939. Arnheim applied methods of psychology to the study of art and esthetic experience.

I.2.7 Wladyslaw Tatarkiewicz (1886–1980), a Polish philosopher, systematized, in his *History of Six Ideas,* the terms *art, beauty, form, creativity, mimesis,* and *esthetic experience*.

I.2.8 Ivan Pavlov (1849–1936), a Russian physiologist, had no research interest in esthetics, but he demonstrated the existence of conditioned reflexes and thus made a significant contribution to the understanding of human response to change in the environment.

I.2.9 Max Wertheimer (1880–1943), a German psychologist, started the Gestalt school of psychology, which stresses studying entire patterns of mental process rather than single sensations.

I.2.10   Abraham H. Maslow (1908–1970), an American psychologist, is known for his work on the process of motivation.

I.2.11   Louis Henri Sullivan (1856–1924), an American architect, originated the battle cry of modern designers: Form Follows Function.

I.2.12   Le Corbusier (1887–1965), a French architect, created *Modulor*, a standard system of measurement derived from the golden mean of proportions of the human body. (See also all commentaries under 1.5).

I.2.13   Walter Gropius (1883–1969), a German architect, the founder (1919) of the Bauhaus, the first school of architecture to teach industrial design.

I.3   The Idea

I.3.1   How can the special relationship between the terms *beauty* and *visual quality* be explained? According to the Short Oxford Dictionary, *beauty* is a "quality ...which affords keen pleasure to the senses, especially that of sight." The importance of sight can, perhaps, be explained by the mainly visual nature of humans. As much as 90 percent of what we know, we learn by seeing (Miller 1965, 15).

When a need arose for naming the facility of nonrational cognition, the word added to the language was *intuition*, which is derived from the Latin *intueri*, to look upon.

Clearly, the faculty of seeing occupies a central position in the spectrum of those faculties indispensable for contact with the outside world. This explains the traditional preoccupation of the discipline of esthetics with visual stimuli.

It is only fair to admit that the above position is not universally accepted. This is particularly true in the field of product esthetics, where it is not uncommon, for instance, to consider the "clunk" of a car door, the smell of a plastic lamp, or the ergonomic properties of a machine (physical fit of machine to human) esthetic stimuli (Warren 1982).

I.3.2 Alfred Damon Runyon (1884–1946), an American journalist and short-story writer. The citation quoted is, of course, a paraphrase of Ecclesiastes 9:11.

I.4 The Presentation

I.4.1 Walter Gropius is quoted in Pawlowski (1965).

Chapter 1. Terms Defined

1.1 Human Needs

1.1.1 Maslow presented his hierarchy of needs in *Motivation and Personality* (1954, 80–92).

1.2 Form

1.2.1 For a discussion of the traditional meanings of the term *form* see Tatarkiewicz (1980, 220–243).

1.2.2 Can *industrial design* be successfully defined as a discipline? The concept of an industrial form in terms of external entries and exits of the technical system of the product was proposed by Czekaluk (1966). Czekaluk was primarily concerned with the boundaries of the discipline of industrial design. He defined the discipline as the design of industrial forms or the process of developing those components of external entries and exits of the product that come into relationship with people during the product's utilization.

1.2.3 The elements of cybernetic terminology have been based on Ashby (1961), Czekaluk (1966), Greniewski (1959) and Wiener (1948).

1.2.4 To simplify this presentation we loosely refer to eyes and ears, for example, as entries of the human biological system. They are in fact material representations of the entries. *Entry* and *exit* have abstract meanings. They do not have weight, hardness, or resilience, as do their material representations.

The table below lists with their material representations the pairs of exits and entries selected from examples of biological and technical systems:

The Form of the Human Biological System

Outside Entries	Material Representations	Outside Exits	Material Representations
Sight	Eye	Voice	Mouth & Throat
Hearing	Ear	Force	Motor System
Smelling	Nose	Appearance	Shape & Color

and so on...

The Form of Radio's Technical System

Outside Entries	Material Representations	Outside Exits	Material Representations
On/Off	Switch	Voice	Speaker
Select	Turn Knob	Sight of Scale	Scale
Volume	Turn Knob	Appearance	Shape & Color

and so on...

1.3 Beauty

1.3.1 A broad review of the history of the term *beauty,* including the sources of its ambiguity, is provided by, among others, Tatarkiewicz (1980).

1.3.2 Collingwood takes an eloquent stand against monopolizing the term *beauty* for esthetics: *beauty* has both an esthetic and a nonesthetic use (1958, 36-41).

1.3.3 According to Morawski, "Since the word *beauty* is a homonym, it also assumes a nonesthetic meaning" (1966, 113).

1.3.4 In the introduction to his *Art and Industry,* Read writes that functional objects will most likely possess esthetic quality though they do not always do so. Functional does not necessarily mean beautiful (1954, 81).

1.3.5 Gropius points out with characteristic acuteness that there is only a half-truth in the belief that fitness for purpose equals beauty: every human face is fit for its purpose, but only some are beautiful (1955, 5).

1.3.6 Arnheim argues in *Toward Psychology of Art* that it is not enough for an object to be functional to be useful (1966, 202). It is necessary that its function be visible. He also writes that "the functional appearance is due to a translation of physical forces into visual language" (ibid., 204). This implies esthetic intervention in the design process.

1.4 Expression

1.4.1 The discussion of "expression" has been based primarily on Arnheim, *Art and Visual Perception* (1966) and *Toward a Psychology of Art* (1966), Collingwood (1958), and Tatarkiewicz (1972).

1.4.2 There is a small problem with expression of industrial products as compared with that of works of arts. Experience in the arts shows that it is better when the expression is not explicit, but rather when feelings are implied or insinuated (Collingwood 1958, 111). In product design, on the contrary, the more unequivocal the industrial form is, the better it is.

The described reservations apply mainly to communication of a visual order and the product's function. At the level of higher needs, expression of industrial forms assumes a role similar to that which it plays in the arts. In this sense, while choosing, shall we say, an automobile, we are not only looking for a means of transportation but also for a way to express our temperament, aspirations, taste, and so on. At this level, some ambiguity may, in fact, be helpful in creating a desired image.

1.4.3 The use of *informativeness* as equivalent to *expression* in the analysis of industrial products is taken from the Soviet researcher Azrikan (1966).

1.5   Esthetic Value and Esthetic Emotion.

1.5.1   This chapter is based on Galecki (1962), Golaszewska (1970), Ingarden (1966), Morawski (1957), Ossowski (1978), Read (1972), Stolnitz (1965), and Tatarkiewicz (1972; 1980).

1.5.2   For more on the "Great Theory," also loosely referred to as "a canon of classical beauty," see Tatarkiewicz (1980, 125). Traced in the works of the craftsmen of ancient Greece, its principles are, primarily, the preference for symmetry, for a straight line, and for proportions of the *golden mean.*

1.5.3   What is the *golden mean?* The proportions of the *golden mean* are governed by the number 1.618. For unknown reasons, a rough approximation of a proportion defined by this number is found everywhere in nature, from the structure of crystals to the build of the human body. For instance, in an adult the distance from the ground to the waist is to the distance from the waist to the top of the head a ratio of approximately 1.6:1.

Starting with a single side of 100 inches, one can build two *golden mean* rectangles: 161.8/100 = 1.618 or 100/61.8 = 1.618. Dividing a 100-inch rod according to this rule produces two pieces of 61.8- and 38.2-inch length respectively (61.8/38.2 = 1.618). Please note that the reciprocity of 1.618 is 0.618.

A peculiar property of this proportion has been mathematically modeled by Fibonacci. Fibonacci number series are sequences where each number is equal to the sum of the two preceding ones. For instance: 61.8, 100, 161.8, 261.8, 423.6, and so on, extending in both directions. In addition, each pair of adjacent numbers remains in the same *golden mean* ratio based on 1.618.

Le Corbusier used Fibonacci series in developing *Modulor,* an architectonic system of standardized measurement based on golden mean proportions found in the human body. Le Corbusier provides several examples of the application of the golden mean in design. For a criticism of *Modulor,* see Arnheim, *Toward a Psychology of Art* (1966, 102).

In practice, hardly anybody adheres religiously to the exact number 1.618; they usually approximate it with 1-2/3 or its rough reciprocal of 2/3.

A designer's propensity for the application of standards such as *Modulor* depends much on creative temperament. Some designers use the rule of the golden mean as a prompter in moments of indecision. Albert Einstein remarked about *Modulor:* "It is a scale of proportions which makes the bad difficult and the good easy" (quoted in Le Corbusier 1980, 58).

1.5.4   For more application of mathematical analysis in the design of visual patterns, see Hambidge (1959).

1.5.5   Gestalt psychology was developed mainly by the German psychologists Wertheimer, Koffka, and Kohler (see Ellis 1950 and Szewczyk 1957). Its application to the analysis of visual arts and architecture was the subject of research by Arnheim, *Art* (1966) and Zorawski (1962), among others.

1.5.6   The principles of Associational Esthetics were developed by the German philosopher G. T. Fechner (1801-1887), but he had several predecessors in Germany, England, and France (Tatarkiewicz 1972, 399-403).

1.5.7   For an in-depth review of Functionalist Theory, see Zurko (1957).

1.5.8   Valentine, analyzing a functional component of esthetic value writes that the original conscious influence of purposeful suitability becomes ultimately "non-explicit, hanging vaguely in the background, and yet contributing...to total judgment and feeling of delight" (1962, 165).

1.5.9   I subscribe to the concept of the unity of human body and psychic faculties directed toward sustaining a satisfying life in all its aspects. This concept is based on a conviction of the biological foundation of esthetic emotions. The quotations below are cited in support of this concept:

> "There is no need for saying that there exist specific esthetic emotions, which would possess characteristics different from those of all other emotions" (Segal 1911, 377).

"There exists some property of the nervous system which determines esthetic judgments, a property which is biologically derived" (Eysenck 1958, 319).

"Esthetic emotion, the sense of beauty and ugliness, takes its beginning in emotion associated with reaching a desired goal…The formation of esthetic emotion gradually displaces the sense of the goal" (Sunderland 1961, 59).

"The process that takes place in the onlooker is emotional: it is accompanied by all the involuntary reflexes which a psychologist would associate with emotion" (Read 1972, 38).

Chapter 2. Esthetic Emotion as Information

2.1 Human Adaptational Activities

2.1.1 The life processes of maintaining the balances of organisms are described in an extensive and readily available literature. The views presented in this book on the subject are based on the following works in the attached bibliography: Cannon (1963), Grayson (1966), Guillaume (1958), Hausmanowa (1955), Hyman (1964), Levit (1981), Maruszewski (1969), Maslow (1954), Miller (1965), Nowacki (1969), Pavlov (1928), Pieter (1963), Szuman (1956), and Traczyk (1969). The references noted represent only a small fraction of the available sources.

2.1.2 A popular dictionary defines *consciousness* as the awareness of oneself and one's surroundings. We will be satisfied with this description since science has not yet been successful in formulating a definition of consciousness that would meet with common acceptance. At best, some level of agreement exists as to components of consciousness such as alertness, memory, concrete and abstract thinking, and the ability to experience sensations and emotions.

2.2 From Simple to Complex Psychological Processes

2.2.1 The example of a machinist (case D) is taken from Nowacki (1969, 151).

2.3   The Human as a Self-regulating System

2.3.1 Wiener, Norbert (1894–1964), an American mathematician, founded the study of cybernetics as the theory of control systems (see Wiener 1948).

2.4   Emotion as an Indicator of Value

2.5   Emotions of Involuntary Behavior

2.5.1 The example of an orange circle is taken from Valentine (1962, 29).

2.5.2 According to Pavlov (1928), even the most complex human activities are reflexes.

2.5.3 The following example illustrates the potential of the transfer of values in shaping responsiveness to visual qualities:

Suppose a young, relatively unknown woman becomes the wife of a prince of the British royal family. The world goes crazy about her. By the very nature of her new social position and her natural attractiveness she seems to have begun to personify all that is best in a model human being: intelligence, courage, poise, you name it. But this is only half of the story. Because of her actual or apparent virtues, which are considered worth imitating, she starts to set worldwide standards of fashion, be it a haircut or a dotted-fabric dress. I am sure that after this occurs for some time, young girls in some parts of the world would consider the specific haircut or dress fashionable even without knowing about the existence of the princess (if this were possible).

What we have witnessed in this case is a conditioned transfer of values from an admired person (a British princess) to visual patterns associated with her (dotted fabrics). Because of this transfer, the dotted patterns become a fashion, temporarily considered more attractive and desirable than any other pattern. I do not hesitate to recommend that anyone involved in product development maintain alertness and sensitivity toward all changes occurring in the visual culture of our times.

2.6 Emotions of Rational Behavior

2.7 Summary on Emotions

2.7.1   It cannot be emphasized too strongly that the dramatic simplification of the diagrams with which we illustrate complex psychological phenomena (figs. 9-12, 14, 15, 16, 20, 25) have been accepted only for the purpose of coming closer to our didactic objectives. Any overconfidence in the application of engineering certainty to an understanding of humans would be a risky proposition.

The diagrams are sketches without pretensions to scientific accuracy—a couple of lines drawn to represent what is "average" in human responses to the outside world. But even while being aware of these limitations we should not forget a warning by Claude Bernard, the French physiologist who, in another context, had already written in 1861:

> "Another ...application of mathematics to biology is the use of averages which, in medicine and physiology, leads, so to speak, necessarily to error. There are doubtless several reasons for this; but the greatest obstacle to applying calculations to physiological phenomena is still, at bottom, the excessive complexity which prevents their being definite and comparable one with another" (1957, 134).

2.8   Life Function of Esthetic Emotions

2.8.1   The idea of a "drive toward life goals" lying at the root of esthetic emotions was persuasively presented by Sunderland (1961).

2.8.2   Baruch Spinoza (1632–1677) has had perhaps the most pervasive influence of all modern philosophers with the possible exception of Immanuel Kant (see commentary I.2.4). Spinoza's thought—"If motion which the nerves receive by means of the eyes from objects before us is conducive to health, those objects are called beautiful"—asserting the role of needs in esthetic experience ostensibly contradicts Kant's views on this subject. The entry "Aesthetics" in Funk & Wagnall's *New Encyclopedia* describes Kant's views as follows: "Objects are judged beautiful when they satisfy a disinterested desire: one that does not involve our personal interest or needs." However, on examination the contradiction disappears, since Spinoza writes about the sources of esthetic emotion and Kant refers to esthetic emotion itself. In other words, Spinoza answers the question why?, while Kant answers the question how?

Esthetic preferences develop as a function of needs. Once the preferences are reinforced, the conscious link of purpose between what is needed and what is liked is erased: appreciation of visual beauty becomes disinterested.

2.8.3   Spinoza is quoted in Durant (1977, 174). In reference to this quotation ("If motion which the nerves receive…"), it is interesting to note that the word *agreeable* in its meaning of "nice, pleasant, giving pleasure" clearly has an esthetic overtone. The adjective *agreeable* takes its root from the verb to *agree*, an acceptance of the influence of something on us or its contact with us.

2.8.4   A cognitive function of esthetic emotion was recognized by Baumgarten, the father of the term *(a)esthetics*. Referring to auditory stimuli, he acknowledged the "unclear" cognizance offered by poetry as opposed to the "clear" cognizance which is characteristic of science (see Morawski 1957, 20).

2.8.5   As shown earlier (chapter 1), the application of cybernetic terminology provides an opportunity for effective, if unconventional, approaches to the meaning of form. The usefulness of the theory of information for our investigation hardly ends there. The closed run of information in the adaptational processes provides a simple framework for the description of human responses to the outside world. It underscores the unity of all the human adaptational activities directed toward preservation and well-being. The concept that esthetic experience is nothing more than one of the family of emotions becomes more convincing than ever. And finally, cybernetic terminology provides us with a methodological isolation of the process of automatic valuation of visual stimuli, and does so with ease and clarity. This valuation is, as has been shown, a springboard for esthetic emotion.

2.8.6 Questions expressing doubts might be asked: Do esthetic emotions really guide us toward what is useful? If so, why don't people with a refined esthetic taste do much better in life then others do? How do we explain an apparent inconsistency between what, on the one hand, our investigation seems to lead us to and, on the other, what at least some of our experience seems to indicate?

Part of the answer lies in the place the word *esthetics* and its derivatives occupy in our everyday language. Is it not true that the term *esthetic experience* is associated with objects and situations as remote from immediate utility as possible? Esthetic experience is a pink carnation in the lapel of a tuxedo, a chamber orchestra tuning its strings before the opening chords of a concert, or the turning of the heavy pages in a rare edition of a lavishly illustrated book. In short, we have a tendency to think of *esthetics* as a term associated with leisure time and indulgence in the arts. In addition, a preoccupation with the arts as a means for making a living usually does not produce, with certain exceptions, an enviable income. On the contrary, the proverbial starving artist fits our understanding much better. Certainly there are other human character traits more effective in achieving success than esthetic sensitivity; courage and persistence come first to mind.

However, there is a branch of esthetics that is beyond art and is the center of our interest: the one focusing on the visual beauty (see commentary I.1.2). Is it not an esthetic emotion that, on a lazy stroll to a fork in the road, turns our steps toward a sunny path into the park and away from that narrow and dark back alley into the slums? No analytical thinking at all might have taken place in weighing the differences: a safe, warm, and airy space on the one side and a narrow, filthy, and dangerous alley on the other. The choice, most likely, has been made involuntarily on the basis of a rapid, subconscious comparison of visual patterns signaling safety and health in one direction and danger and illness in the other.

Is it not an esthetic emotion that determines that the last plate to be picked up from the stack in a cafeteria will be the one, otherwise perfect, that has a small crack at the edge?

So it is in this sense that esthetic emotions accompany all our actions and influence all our choices. I believe that esthetic experiences are commonplace. They are so much an ordinary and everyday experience that someone reminded about it might justifiably express a surprise similar to that of Monsieur Jourdan, the hero in a comedy by Moliere, who was amazed to learn that he spoke in prose.

Do esthetic emotions really guide us toward what is useful? It very much depends on what *utility* means to each individual. Sometimes a need to appear more affluent makes one rent an apartment in a fancy neighborhood and sleep on the floor because of a lack of additional money for furniture. In this case a need to appear well-to-do is more important than sleeping comfortably. No matter what someone's esthetic preferences are, it could be difficult to prove that any of them are actually directed against that person's needs, even if they are only perceived needs.

2.8.7   Our immediate attraction to a good-looking member of the opposite sex is a good example of esthetic values at work. The evidence of an attractive appearance is imprecise but our positive reaction is instantaneous. When more information about a person who has come to our attention becomes available, our preliminary impression will be either reinforced or modified negatively (Sunderland 1961, 59).

2.8.8   Is it possible that the division of emotional responses into "inborn" and "acquired" corresponds with what philosophical esthetics identifies as "objective" values on the one hand and "subjective" on the other?

If all of us respond in the same way toward an object shown to us, the suspicion is that our response is inborn, that it is typical of the way the species has developed and the way it acts. Was it this predictability, this sureness of response that created the belief that some esthetic values are objectively the characteristic of observed visual patterns?

It is much easier, of course, to establish a link between acquired emotional responses and their individual, subjective character.

2.8.9 We have analyzed the informative value of emotions. Could it be that the capacity for emotional experience also plays the role of a peculiar "shock absorber," which slows down the formation of new habits, new patterns of involuntary behavior? We sometimes say, I cannot bring myself to do this or that. The conditioned patterns of responses moderate our conduct. People who change their behavior continually are considered erratic and irresponsible.

The stability of reflexes and of the emotions that are associated with these reflexes are likely responsible for the inertia observed in the development of new esthetic preferences.

Chapter 3. Esthetic Values of Industrial Products

3.1   X, Y, and Z Esthetic Values

3.1.1   It is possible to hypothesize that, when filtered through the meaning of human needs, to which the product designer is obliged to respond, the various existing theories of esthetic experience (Gestalt, Functionalist, and so on) simply apply to different components of human sensitivity to esthetic stimuli.

3.1.2   I had some hesitation as to the proper designation of the three major groups of esthetic values, but finally settled on the letters X, Y, and Z. Graphically, the homogeneity of the design of these letters projects the sense of the bond that exists between the three values, the unity of esthetic response. However, the reader may find it helpful to know that there was a competing set of letters under consideration: the letters O, F, and C. The logic behind this alternative choice is evident in the comparison presented below:

X.....................O for (**O**)rder
Y.....................F for (**F**)unction
Z.....................C for (**C**)ulture

3.2   Block X: Visual Order as Esthetic Value

3.2.1   Gestalt psychology is not immune to criticism. The substance of such criticism really goes beyond the scope of this book. The interested reader can find information on the Gestalt controversy in Allport (1961), Ellis (1950), and Kanizsa (1966) among other references. Whatever the criticism may be, there seems to be a general agreement as to the validity of the experimental findings of the Gestaltists.

3.2.2   For more on the meaning of visual simplicity see Arnheim, *Art* (1966, 45-49).

3.2.3   It is interesting to note in respect to block X esthetic values that the obviously esthetic qualification contained in the word *neat* has a clear connection with order and clarity.

3.3   Synthesizing Tendencies of Perception

3.3.1   Allport (1961, 113) indicates that there have been more than a hundred Gestalt rules formulated by various writers. In many cases, however, those rules restate one another or provide corollaries rather than actually adding to the concept of "good" form. It is difficult to avoid a degree of repetitiveness while formulating even as few as eight synthesizing tendencies of perception.

3.3.2   In respect to the tendency toward geometrizing and creating visual organization on a grid of straight lines, there exists a strong body of evidence provided by Gestalt psychology that these propensities are inborn rather than conditioned. See, among others, the works of Arnheim, *Art* (1966, 35) and Zorawski (1962, 25).

3.3.3 The use of the unifying tendency of straight lines by designers as far back as ancient Greece has been noted by many authors, among them Le Corbusier (1980), Teague (1940), and Zorawski (1962).

3.3.4 "Unity in diversity" is one of the resilient, intuitively formulated ideas of beauty. Gestalt experiments with homogeneity, rhythm, symmetry, and so on, seem to confirm the existence of a preference for such a regularity in the mechanism of perception.

3.3.5 The value of geometrizing and of a straight line in design may sometimes be misunderstood. This value really should not be equated with a necessity for good forms to be sharp, edgy, "uncuddly." Rather, the value applies to the basic outline of the form, its main design axes, or its esthetic directive (compare figs. 40, 43, 51C). It was only in this sense that the French painter Cezanne could insist that the world consists of cubes, spheres, cylinders, and cones. In Cezanne's convention, the human head is a sphere, the trunk of the body a cylinder, and so on.

3.3.6 Paul Cezanne (1839-1906), a French painter, exerted a great influence on modern art.

3.3.7 Karen Blixen, an alert and sensitive observer, writing under the pen name of Isak Dinesen, reminisces:

"In the wildness and irregularity of the country, a piece of land laid out and planned according to rule, looked very well. Later on, when I flew in Africa, and became familiar with the appearance of my farm from the air, I was filled with admiration for my coffee-plantation, that lay quite bright green in the gray-green land, and *I realized how keenly the human mind yearns for geometrical figures.*" (Emphasis mine. Quoted from Isak Dinesen's *Out of Africa*. New York: Vintage Books, 1985, p. 7).

3.4 Block Y: Functionalism as Esthetic Value

3.4.1 Here is an example of a functional design that was developed the way an organic form would develop: An engineer faced the problem of finding the lowest hydroresistance for one of the first submarines to be constructed and did so without the benefit of either mathematical analysis or a test laboratory, neither being yet available. The engineer made a crude, scaled-down approximation of the boat's hull out of a solid block of sugar, then immersed it in a stream of water. The stream dissolved first those fragments of the carving where the pressure of the water—and therefore the hydroresistance of the model hull—was the highest. After a couple of minutes of allowing the water to work on the sugar, the engineer had a hydro-dynamically correct model to follow in design.

3.4.2 An indispensable source for studying the functionalist theory is the work of Zurko (1957).

3.4.3 Substantiation of the esthetic value of functionality is given by, among other authors, Arnheim *Toward a Psychology* (1966, 192-211), Ossowski (1978), and Valentine (1962, 165).

3.4.4 It would be difficult to contradict such a statement, as "surely there are objects that are functional but ugly." But how can we explain it? Let us point to a couple of major reasons:

— Total esthetic value has more components than just the functionality of the object. For instance, an object may be functional and its visual organization chaotic.

— The functionality of the object can be poorly communicated. The funnel-shaped entrance to a ski holder (ref. section 1.4, Expression) was "inviting." Such a shape communicated well the function of accepting the skis. The form had some "excess" of functionality. A blunt entrance in this case would communicate the function less persuasively.

— There has to be some appreciation of the functionality of the object based on the viewer's experience. For instance, possessing a mechanical aptitude increases the viewer's esthetic enjoyment of well-designed tools.

3.5   Universal Appeal of Functionality

3.5.1   The German psychologist Lipps was the first to notice the connection between the actions of the human body and our learning the laws of balance and movement from them (see Slawinska 1969, 22).

3.5.2   The naming of machine components after parts of the human body was discussed by Ashford (1966, 58-59).

3.5.3   The example of children playing with toys is taken from Slawinska (1969, 22).

3.5.4   Perhaps, it is not asking too much to pose the question once more: When does the functional become esthetic? To acquire esthetic meaning, the functional has to become familiar to the point that its recognition becomes automatic. A visually communicated "excess" of functionality helps esthetic appreciation.

3.6   Visual Symbolism of Function

3.6.1   While translating the function of the product into visual language, the designer will most likely refer to a particular class of visual symbols rather then to a concrete, individual object (see Vernon 1965, 31).

3.6.2   The visualization of dynamism and movement has been largely based on Arnheim, *Art* (1966, 397).

3.6.3   For more on visual balance see Arnheim, *Art* (1966, 9) and Valentine (1962, 93).

3.6.4   "The striving for balance can be described as a striving for simplicity. By eliminating ambiguity and disunity, balance increases the simplicity of a composition"(Arnheim, *Art* 1966, 52).

3.7   Form and Function

3.7.1   The example of the bridges was supplied by Jadwiga Slawinska.

3.7.2 The idea of an "excess of functionality" gaining "decorative autonomy" is taken from Sandauer (1957, 22).

3.7.3 With respect to the "excess of functionality," Arnheim notes that galloping horses are frequently painted with legs outstretched beyond what is naturally possible but in a way that emphasizes the direction and dynamism of movement (*Art* 1966, 408). Even the proof demonstrated by photography would not convince the painters to change the design. They know, and they are right, that movement is better translated into visual language through the application of some "excess" of functionality. However, caution is well advised. Too much of the "excess" leads to caricature.

3.7.4 With all respect for the powerful, culture-shaping effect of Sullivan's "form follows function," some of us feel today that truth might be better served if the battle cry of modern designers was modified to "form should emphasize function." And perhaps what Sullivan really had in mind was not that function determines the form but simply that function has priority over form for objects utility. Such an interpretation clearly leaves room for esthetic intervention in design.

3.7.5 People who make products for a living hardly share the agony of some theoretically inclined minds: Is it OK to apply esthetic criteria in judging a utilitarian object or not? In the May 1987 issue of *Car and Driver* in an article characteristically entitled "Form Follows Fashion," Yasushi Ishiwatari wrote that "Honda has unveiled a restyled City car with a lower and wider shape. When we asked Nobuhiko Kawamoto, the head of Honda R&D, why the company made the change, he replied simply, 'Because it looks better.'"

3.7.6 William Ockham (1285–?1349), was an English philosopher and an Franciscan monk. The principle of "Ockham's razor" in application to design was presented by Teague (1940, 408).

3.8 Block Z: Responsiveness to the Prevailing Visual Taste

3.8.1 The trend in design of following the forms of technological leaders (aircraft, computers, and so on) was noted, among other authors, by Mayall (1967, 105).

3.8.2 The concept of the sexual foundations of esthetic preferences was one of the ideas researched by Freud (see Valentine 1962, 21-22). Despite the shared characteristics of a basic psychological drive, sexual aspects of esthetic taste represent various and fluctuating qualities, depending on the gender of the subject, on the subject's position in society, and on community standards.

3.8.3 Skinner's experiments have been described in Hyman (1964, 85-86).

3.8.4 The affinity of all industrial products with the "technological leaders" was noted by, among other writers, Mayall (1967, 105).

3.8.5 A dramatic example of the transfer of cultural values in forming esthetic preferences can be found in the behavior of an African tribe. The tribe's young women have their front teeth brutally removed in an evident attempt to look more attractive, and these efforts are obviously appreciated by the local men. Upon investigation, this seemingly bad taste can be simply explained. It happens that the tribe's most valued possession is its herd of cows. Cows do not have front teeth and, hence, a black hole in place of healthy front teeth has come to represent something to look for or even to be desired.

3.8.6 Frank Lloyd Wright (1867-1959), was a pioneer in modern American architecture. In his concept of "organic architecture" he taught that buildings should develop out of their natural surroundings.

3.9 Transitions of Culture

3.9.1 Baruch's anecdote is quoted in Mackay (1980, xiii).

3.9.2 T. S. Eliot's reflection on the discipline of esthetics is quoted in Stolnitz (1965, 1).

3.10 Esthetic Mediation in the Design Process

3.10.1 Those who oppose esthetic intervention in engineering design have forgotten that esthetic decisions are made automatically, irrespective of our will. The question is not whether esthetic considerations should be allowed in product design but how to optimize their influence.

3.10.2 In a well-run design office, taking care of the visual quality of the product can be pretty much controlled, as opposed to allowing it to follow the whims of creativity. A manager of a design office shares his experience on this subject:

"Every few years we take our company through the process of establishing the 'company look,' a specific 'design idiom.' Our product is electronic office equipment. First, we prepare a questionnaire to be answered by our management people. How do they see our product development philosophy? What makes our presence on the market strong?

"We examine the questionnaires and make a list of those adjectives which appear with the greatest frequency. Suppose that the list runs as follows: 'Conservative—reliable—refined—friendly—high tech.' These adjectives are representative of an image we want to project in the market.

"Now, we have a brain-storming session in the design office. How to translate the desired image into the visual language of design? At the end of the session we have short notes for each adjective on the list. Here, for instance, is how we are going to project 'reliability':

— 'Thick' panels that look solid, unbreakable
— Conservative colors
— Square or golden mean proportions
— Horizontal emphasis rather than vertical
— Appearance of having a low center of gravity
— Simple forms
— No thin edges or small parts that look as if they could get knocked off or broken
— Broad reveal lines between panels make the panels look easy to open
— Obvious openings for servicing

"We do a similar exercise with the other parameters of our 'design idiom.' Now we have a guide in our hands for all our designers to follow. The method is crude but we get results."

3.10.3 In respect to the purposefulness of esthetic decisions in design, typical testimony is provided by the Polish architect Hryniewiecki. He recognizes that the multitude of special requirements makes it difficult for the designer to optimize the design. Equally difficult is reaching the best decision at a forum of specialists. In such a situation, an esthetic criterion acquires a special importance: "Esthetic assessment of the created design affords the simplest and usually the soundest decision in respect to the direction in which the architectonic form should develop" (1966, 237).

3.10.4 The search for an attractive industrial form is so exciting partly because it demands the reconciliation of several competing pairs of requirements. The inertia in the pattern of human emotional responses (see commentary 2.8.9) competes with curiosity about the new. The visual excess of functionality is moderated by the demands of simplicity. The tendency to camouflage is countered by the requirements of the communicativeness of the form. Special talent for both analysis and synthesis in design is essential for a successful designer.

3.10.5 With all the information provided it would be unfair to compare this book with a typical reference product-design manual. While the performance of the product or its strength can be calculated and tested, the visual quality can be measured only by the response it receives in the competitive market. Certainly this happens when the product has already been designed.

3.11 Summary

3.11.1 In response to the pivotal questions of this book we can now formulate the following answers:

Question 1: What are the esthetic values of the industrial product?

Answer: They are those characteristics of its form that, at the mere sight of the product, generate spontaneous, positive emotions on the part of the beholder.

Question 2: What are the components of the esthetic value of industrial products?

Answer:

X: the visual order of the elements of its form

Y: the visual pattern of its form that communicates and emphasizes the function of the product

Z: the visual symbolism expressing the product's affinity with the culture of the time

Question 3: What features of the industrial product possess esthetic merit?

Answer: Shape, color, hue and intensity, surface texture, and the visual relationships among these components.

Question 4: What distinguishes esthetic emotion from other emotions generated by contact with the industrial product?

Answer: Esthetic emotion can be described by the following set of parameters:

Faculty: Seeing
Object: Form
Attitude: Disinterested
Structure: Reflex

Question 5: There is a traditional distrust of any formal prescriptions for creating esthetic value. Can a theory of esthetic value be presented without stated formulas?

Answer: It is believed that the approach suggested in this book enriches strategic choices of design and does not demand the following of any particular formula.

3.11.2 Is it necessary, while investigating the issues of product esthetics, to resort to the ideas of the adaptational feedback loop, reflex, conditioning, reward and punishment in learning, and so on? Is not a reference to psychology and the theory of information creating an undue burden in understanding the subject?

I may only address such a potential criticism in the following way:

The chosen approach is certainly not the only one possible. It is not even the prevailing one in the literature of the subject. In my personal view, such a situation is disappointing for the product designer.

At the level of esthetic intervention in product design today, "gut feeling" predominates. Currently reigning in the critical analysis of the products' visual beauty is "good taste," which resorts to the instinct for "right form." I am far from underrating the role that instinct plays not only in design but in the critical evaluation of design as well. But I have always believed that some measure of discipline is possible in the pursuit of the esthetic value in product design. Further, it has become apparent to me that such a goal would not be achieved without first explaining how humans pursue their life goals and how they behave in a changing environment. I now firmly believe that only by resorting to such a background is it possible to explain the ability to appreciate visual beauty not as some freak characteristic of human faculties but as one solidly rooted in the human capacity for life, growth, and survival.

Finally, borrowing models from psychology and the theory of information allows for the experiment of systemizing the issues of product esthetics in a way approximating the methods employed by industry. This applies to setting goals and establishing procedures. It is believed that a lot of preliminary hesitation and indecision in design can be avoided by adopting the XYZ concept of esthetic values as it is presented here. This will hopefully cut down on the cost of product development and will increase the chances of introducing an attractive product into the market.

Bibliography

Adler, M. J. *Six Great Ideas*. New York: Collier Books, 1984.

Allport, F. G. *Theories of Perception and the Concept of Structure*. New York: John Wiley & Sons, 1961.

Arnheim, R. *Art and Visual Perception*. Berkeley: University of California Press, 1966.

---. *Toward a Psychology of Art*. Berkeley: University of California Press, 1966.

---. *Visual Thinking*. Berkeley: University of California Press, 1969.

Ashby, W. R. *Introduction to Cybernetics*. New York: John Wiley & Sons, 1961.

Ashford, F. C. *Designing for Industry*. London: Sir Isaac Pitman and Sons, 1955.

---. "Visual Organization." *Design* 213 (1966).

---. *The Esthetics of Engineering Design*. London: Business Book, 1969.

Azrikan, D. "Informativeness of Form: Indispensable Condition of its Esthetic Excellence." Moscow: *Tekhnicheskaya Estietika* 2 (1966).

Bayley S., Philippe Gardner, and Deyan Sudjic. *Style and Design*. New York: Van Norstrand Reinhold, 1986.

Bernard, C. *An Introduction to the Study of Experimental Medicine*. New York: Dover, 1957.

Bill, M. *Form*. Basel: Karl Werner, 1952.

Cannon, W. B. *The Wisdom of the Body*. New York: Norton Library, 1963.

Cataldo, J. W. *Graphic Design and Visual Communications*. Scranton: International Text Book, 1966.

Collingwood, R. D. *The Principles of Art*. New York: Oxford University Press, 1958.

Croce, B. *Zarys Estetyki* (Esthetics). Warsaw: PWN, 1961.

Czekaluk, B. "O Pojeciu Formy" (On the meaning of form). Warsaw: *Wiadomosci IWP* 11-12 (1965) and 1-2 (1966).

Dember, W. N., and J. S. Warm. *Psychology of Perception*. New York: Holt, Rinehart, and Winston, 1979.

Downer, M. *Discovering Design*. New York: Lothorp, Lee, and Shepard, 1947.

Durant, W. *The Story of Philosophy*. New York: Pocket Books, 1977.

Ellis, W. D. *A Source Book of Gestalt Psychology*. London: Routledge & Kegan, 1950.

Eysenck, H. J. *Sense and Nonsense in Psychology*. Middlesex: Penguin Books, 1958.

Francastel, P. *Sztuka i Technika* (Art and technology). Warsaw: PWN, 1966.

Galecki, J. *Problematyka Estetyki* (The subject of esthetics). Krakow: Wydawnictwo Literackie, 1962.

Gibson, J. J. *The Senses Considered as Perceptual Systems*. Westport, Conn.: Greenwood Press, 1966.

Golaszewska, M. *Swiadomosc Piekna* (Awareness of beauty). Warsaw: PWN, 1970.

Grayson, J. *Nerwy i Mozg Lodzki* (Nerves and the brain). Warsaw: PWN, 1966.

Gregory, R. L. *Eye and Brain*. London: World University Library, 1967.

Greniewski, H. *Elementy Cybernetyki* (Elements of cybernetics). Warsaw: PWN, 1959.

Grillo, P. J. *Form, Function & Design*. New York: Dover, 1975.

Gropius, W. *Scope of Total Architecture*. New York: Harper and Brothers, 1955.

Guillaume, P. *Podrecznik Psychologii* (Handbook of psychology). Warsaw: PWN, 1958.

Hambidge, J. *The Elements of Dynamic Symmetry*. New Haven: Yale University Press, 1959.

Hausmanowa, J. *Wybrane Zagadnienia Wyzszych Czynnosci Nerwowych* (Some problems of the physiology of higher nervous activities). Warsaw: PZWS, 1955.

Hillier, B. *The Style of the Century, 1900-1980*. New York: E. P. Dutton, 1983.

Hryniewiecki, J. "Architektura Czyli Estetyka Samej Materii" (Architecture as esthetics of the matter itself). Warsaw: *Studia Estetyczne,* Vol. III (1966), 233-247.

Hyman, R. *The Nature of Psychological Inquiry*. Englewood Cliffs, N. J.: Prentice-Hall, 1964.

Ingarden, R. *Przezycie, Dzielo, Wartosc* (Experience, work, value). Krakow: Wydawnictwo Literackie, 1966.

Kanizsa, G. *Organization of Vision*. New York: Praeger, 1966.

Le Corbusier. *The Modulor*. Cambridge: Harvard University Press, 1980.

Levit, R. A. *Physiological Psychology*. New York: Holt, Rinehart and Winston, 1981.

Lewalski, Z. M. "Estetyka Wyrobu Przemyslowego a Jego Wyraz Zewnetrzny" (Esthetic value and expression in industrial products). Warsaw: *Biuletyn Rady Wzornictwa i Estetyki Produkcji* (1965).

---. "Piekno Wyrobu Przemyslowego a Jego Wyraz Zewnetrzny" (Beauty of the industrial product versus its appearance). Warsaw: *Wiadomosci IWP* 3-4 (1966).

---. "Uwagi o Pojeciu Estetyki Wyrobu Przemyslowego" (On the esthetic value of the industrial product). Warsaw: *Wiadomosci IWP* 7-8 (1966).

---. "Estetyka Wyrobow Przemyslowych" (Product esthetics). Warsaw: *Zeszyty Problemowe Przegladu Technicznego* 4 (1968).

Mackay, C. *Extraordinary Popular Delusions and the Madness of Crowds*. New York: Harmony Books, 1980.

McKim, R. H. *Experiments in Visual Thinking*. Monterey, Calif.: Brooks/Cole, 1972.

Maruszewski, M., J. Reykowski, and T. Tomaszewski. *Psychologia Jako Nauka o Czlowieku* (Psychology as a science about man). Warsaw: KIW, 1969.

Maslow, A. H. *Motivation and Personality*. New York: Harper and Brothers, 1954.

Mayall, W. H. *Industrial Design for Engineers*. London: London Illiffe Books, 1967.

Miller, J. G. *The Human Mind*. New York: Golden Press, 1965.

Minsky, M. *The Society of Mind*. New York: Simon and Schuster, 1986.

Morawski, S. *Rozwoj Mysli Estetycznej od Herdera do Heinego* (Evolution of esthetic thought from Herder to Heine). Warsaw: PWN, 1957.

---. *"O Pieknie"* (On beauty). Przeglad Humanistyczny 5 (1966).

Munro, T. *Toward Science in Aesthetics*. New York: Liberal Arts Press, 1956.

Nowacki, T. *Elementy Psychologii* (Elements of psychology). Warsaw: Ossolineum, 1969.

Ossowski, A. *The Foundations of Esthetics*. Boston: D. Ridel, 1978.

Papanek, V. *Design for Human Scale*. New York: Van Norstrand Reinhold, 1983.

Pavlov, I. *Lectures on Conditioned Reflexes*. New York: International Publishers, 1928.

Pawlowski, A. *Zagadnienia Ksztalcenia Plastycznego Dla Potrzeb Wzornictwa Przemyslowego* (Teaching art to the industrial designer). Warsaw: Institute of Industrial Design, 1965.

Pieter, J. *Przedmiot i Metoda Psychologii* (The subject and method of psychology). Warsaw: Ossolineum, 1963.

---. *Sporne Problemy Psychologii* (Controversial problems in psychology). Warsaw: PWN, 1969.

Pininfarina, S. et al. *Function Versus Appearance in Vehicle Design*. Warrendale, Pa.: Society of Automotive Engineers, 1978.

Read, H. *Art and Industry*. New York: Horizon Press, 1954.

---. *The Meaning of Art*. London: Faber & Faber, 1972.

Rock, I. *The Logic of Perception*. Cambridge, Mass: MIT Press, 1983.

Saarinen, E. *The Search for Form in Art and Architecture*. New York: Dover, 1985.

Sandauer, A. *O Jednosci Tresci i Formy* (On the unity of substance and form). Krakow: Wydawnictwo Literackie, 1957.

Santayana, G. *The Sense of Beauty*. New York: Modern Library, 1965.

Schiff, W. *Perception: An Applied Approach*. Boston: Houghton Mifflin, 1980.

Segal, J. "O Charakterze Psychologicznym Zasadniczych Zagadnien Estetycznych" (On the psychological nature of the basic problems of esthetics). Warsaw: *Przeglad Filozoficzny* (1911).

Shigley, J. E., and L. D. Mitchel. *Mechanical Engineering Design*. New York: McGraw Hill, 1983.

Silverman, R. E. *Psychology*. New York: Appleton-Century-Crofts, 1972.

Slawinska, J. *Expresja Sil w Nowoczesnej Architekturze* (The expression of forces in modern architecture). Warsaw: Arkady, 1969.

---. *Estetyka Jako Integralna Dyscyplina Tworczosci Projektanckiej* (Esthetics as an integral discipline of design). Wroclaw, Poland: Wroclaw Polytechnic, 1973.

Stolnitz, J. *Esthetics*. New York: Macmillan, 1965

Sunderland, J. "Geneza Piekna" (Origins of beauty). Warsaw: *Estetyka* (1961).

Szczepanski, S. *Rysunek i Malarstwo* (Drawing and painting). Warsaw: Arkady, 1955.

Szewczyk, W. *Teoria Postaci i Psychologia Postaci* (Theory and psychology of Gestalt). Warsaw: PWN, 1957.

Szuman, S. *Zagadnienia Psychologii Uczuc w Swietle Nauki Pawlowa* (Psychology of emotion in the light of Pavlov's theory). Poznan, Poland: PWN, 1956.

Tatarkiewicz, W. *Droga Przez Estetyke* (The path of esthetics). Warsaw: PWN, 1972.

---. *A History of Six Ideas: An Essay in Esthetics*. The Hague: Martinus Nijhoff, 1980.

Teague, W. D. *Design This Day*. New York: Harcourt, Brace and Co., 1940.

Tomaszewski, T. *Wstep do Psychologii* (Introduction to Psychology). Warsaw: PWN, 1963.

Traczyk, W. *Fizjologiczny Mechanizm Popedow and Emocji* (Physiological mechanism of impulses and emotions). Warsaw: PWN, 1967.

Valentine, C. W. *The Experimental Psychology of Beauty*. London: Methuen, 1962.

Vernon, M. D. *The Psychology of Perception*. London: University of London Press, 1965.

Warren, J. "Styling the Product." *Design Engineering* (August 1982).

Wessel J., and N. Westerman. *American Design Classics*. New York: Design Publications, 1985.

Wiener, N. *Cybernetics*. New York: John Wiley & Sons, 1948.

Wojnar, I. *Perspektywy Wychowawcze Sztuki* (The educational perspectives of art). Warsaw: Nasza Ksiegarnia, 1966.

Zorawski, J. *O Budowie Formy Architektonicznej* (The structure of architectonic form). Warsaw: Arkady, 1962.

Zurko, E. R. *Origins of Functionalist Theory*. New York: Columbia, 1957.

The Sources of Illustrations

All illustrations by the author. Unless otherwise indicated, the sources of the illustrations were also provided by the author. Every effort has been made to identify and credit other sources and the author apologizes for any omissions caused through difficulty in tracing such sources. The author would be grateful to hear from any unacknowledged source.

(23) F-20 Tigershark. Based on a photograph by Jeff Zwart.
(29) Based on figure from R. Arnheim, *Art and Visual Perception*, p. 56.
(31) Based on figure from R. Arnheim, *Art and Visual Perception*, p. 47.
(35) Source unknown.
(36) Source unknown.
(37) Lathe built by Mondiale, industrial design consultant: Societe Technes. Based on a photograph from W. H. Mayall, *Industrial Design for Engineers*, p. 49.
(39) After G. Kanizsa, *Organization in Vision*, p. 100.
(40) Source unknown.
(41) Source unknown.
(42) After Marion Downer, *Discovering Design* (New York: Lothorp, Lee and Shepard, 1947).
(43) 1987 Volvo 740 Turbo.
(44) Based on an example from J. Zorawski, *The structure of Architectonic Form*;
(45) Source unknown.
(46) Source unknown.
(47) 1987 Oldsmobile Toronado. Based on a photograph by Vic Huber.
(48) Source unknown.
(51) Source unknown.
(52) *Top*, ca. 1915 Ford; *bottom*, 1962 Fiat 500.

(53)   Source unknown.

(54)   Source unknown.

(55)   The author's folding bicycle. Manufacturer unknown.

(56A) Michelangelo's Piazza del Campidoglio, Rome, 1546-1564, as analyzed by Le Corbusier in *The Modulor*.

(56B) Based on an analysis from J. Zorawski, *The Structure of Architectonic Form*, p. 92.

(56C) Mercedes Benz sedan. Analyzed by the author.

(56D) From F. C. Ashford, *The Esthetics of Engineering Design*, p. 116.

(57)   1987 Suzuki.

(58)   Based on Michelangelo's *The Battle of Cascina*, 1505.

(64)   1980 Canadian high-speed LRC diesel locomotive by MLW, Alcan and Dofasco.

(65)   Based on S. Szczepanski, *Drawing and Painting*.

(70)   From a temple on the Greek island of Aegina.

(71)   Based on the design by Kenneth Grange for Kenwood, 1950s and 1960s.

(72)   1987 Honda Accord.

(73)   1987 AMC Jeep.

(74)   *Top, Mercedez Benz; bottom*, Lamborghini Countach (as photographed by Jeff Zwart).

(75)   Source unknown.

(78A) From W. Hensel, *Art in Paleolithic Societies* (Warsaw: PWN, 1957), p. 122.

(78B) From N. G. L. Hammond, *A History of Greece* (Oxford: The Clarendon Press, 1967).

(79C) From the catalog of the exhibition "China, Treasures and Splendors." Montreal, 1986.

(79D) From Julius E. Lips, "Vom Ursprung der Dinge."

(80)   From the study of Tandem Computers, Silicon Valley, California, 1986.

(81)   *Left*, Casio watch, 1986; *right* Movado Museum watch, 1987, designed by George Horwitt in 1961.

(82)   An agricultural four-wheel-drive tractor. Versatile Corporation, Winnipeg, Manitoba, 1979. Morley Smith, industrial design consultant; Mark Oleski, project engineer.

(83A) Egyptian stone tool (4000 B.C.). Based on a photograph from W. D. Teague, *Design This Day*.

(83B) Contemporary utility knife. Source unknown.

(84) Source unknown.

(86) Based on a photograph from F. G. Clark and Arthur Gibson, *Concorde* (New York: Crescent Books).

(87) McIntosh 47 sail yacht.

(88) Source unknown.

(89) 1987 Honda Scooter.

(90) *Top*, a motor yacht by Denison; *bottom*, an ocean cruiser, source unknown.

(92) Source unknown.

(93) *Top*, a sewing machine designed by Giorgio Giugiaro for Necchi, 1982; *bottom*, a sewing machine designed by Gio Ponti for Ideal Standard, 1954.

(94) Candleholder on the left based on a photograph from Geoffrey Warren, *Art Nouveau* (London: Octopus Books, 1972); candleholder on the right: source unknown.

(95) Lamp on the left from Geoffrey Warren, *Art Nouveau*; lamp on the right: source unknown.

(96) Based on a photograph by Mark Meyer.

(97) Industrial design by Jim Shook for FMC.

(98) Based on a painting by Syd Mead, from Strother MacMinn, *Syd Mead - Futurist* (Netherlands: A Drago's Dream Book, 1979).

(99) Faucet by Consulate bath appliances.

(100) Source unknown.

(101) Coffee table designed by Isamu Noguchi, manufactured by Herman Miller, 1945.

(102) Tricycle developed by Sinclair Vehicles Ltd, UK, 1985.

(103) Industrial design by Syd Mead for Philips Electronics, Holland.

(104) Source unknown.

(105) Source unknown.

(106) *Top*, a linear tracking turntable, product designer Rick Blanchard; manufacturer: Matsushita Electric Industrial, 1982; *bottom*, a radio amplifier-tuner designed by Jakob Jensen for Bang & Olufsen, Denmark, ca. 1970.

(107) Source unknown.

(108) Personal computer by Epson, 1986.

(109) From the Pontiac–General Motors design office. Industrial design by Jim Shook, early 1970s.

(110) Prototype taxi developed by Guillon, Smith, Marquart & Associates, Montreal.

(111) Light-rail vehicle designed and manufactured by Boeing/Vertol, 1970s.

(112) West Berlin mass transit, heavy-rail vehicle, 1986.

(113) Industrial design by Jim Shook for FMC.

(114) Industrial design by Jim Shook for Bolens.

(115) Based on projects by Jim Shook.

(116) By the author at the Institute of Industrial Design, Warsaw, Poland, 1967.

(117) By the author.

(118) By the author.

(119) By the author, at the Institute of Industrial Design, Warsaw, Poland, 1968.

(120) By the author, at the Institute of Industrial Design, Warsaw, Poland, 1968.

(121) Design by Giorgio Giugiaro, 1986.

(122) Project engineer, Joe Lewalski; industrial design, Jim Shook.

(123) Project engineer, Joe Lewalski; Industrial design, Jim Shook.

(124) Design by the author.

(125) Design by the author.

Index

A Parting Word to the Reader

Now that you have finally arrived at the end of the book, I hope that you have enjoyed it at least in part as much as I enjoyed working on it.

My motivation was divided between the needs for self-clarification and communication. In both of these motivating factors the presence of others was essential, and the exciting atmosphere of the design office influenced me as much as my readings. The experience of designers and engineers had a bearing on my thoughts equal to the works of theoreticians. The importance of interaction with others in writing this book cannot be exaggerated. It is perhaps correct to say that it has been written together with those to whom it is addressed:

— **Product designers**
— **Design engineers**
— **Product development managers**
— **Product planners**
— **Marketing personnel**
— **Product inventors**

I hope this book will undergo the scrutiny of as many practitioners of design as possible. Several types of professionals outside the industry can also benefit from the book and contribute to a critique of it:

— **Architects and interior designers**
— **Book designers and illustrators**
— **Visual advertising designers**
— **Stage and screen designers**
— **Instructors at schools for the visual arts**

And then there is **the public.** After all, we design for ordinary people. Should we not carefully listen to those who are buying our products? Besides, ordinary homes, workrooms, and workshops provide the broadest stage for testing the principles of practical esthetics in action. The affluence of industrial society, the relative ease of acquiring things, and the availability of free time—all encourage individual experiments in visual creativity. Designing one's own home, planning an arrangement of the furniture, choosing one's clothing, decorating the office, doing small exercises in freehand drawing, modeling in clay, taking photographs, and so on, provide all of us with endless opportunities for testing the ways of creative expression. This is the democracy of the arts.

A wide audience would increase the chances of receiving a response. The purpose of these parting words is to make an appeal to the reader: Please, share your thoughts and ideas with me. Do you agree with the book? Do you know good examples of design to support it? Can you offer other examples that contradict the book's conclusions? Have any of the ideas been poorly communicated? Does the language of the book seem easy or difficult? Have you found the book helpful in your design practice? Your criticism as well as support will be highly appreciated.

I am looking forward to your response. **We have written this book together; let's improve it together.**

Please write to:

Design & Development Engineering Press, P. O. Box 3688, Carson City, Nevada 89702

Order Form

To Order *Product Esthetics,* please fill out the order form below and mail it with a check or money order payable to D & D ENGINEERING PRESS. Please allow six to eight weeks for delivery. Money-back guarantee if the book is returned undamaged within 10 days of receipt. **Payment (check or money order) in full must accompany all orders.** Foreign orders must be accompanied by International Money Orders in American dollars only. This offer is valid through December 31, 1990

Please send ____ copy(ies) of *Product Esthetics* @$17.95_____

Shipping $3.00, foreign order $4.00, _____

$0.50 for shipping each additional volume_____

Total enclosed $ _____

Name _____
(Please print)

Address _____

City _____ State _____ Zip _____

Design & Development Engineering Press, P. O. Box 3688, Carson City, Nevada 89702, USA

PRODUCT ESTHETICS
Production Notes

This book was produced by a series of micro computer programs and methods. It was initially typed on a Kapro™ computer by the author using the Wordstar™ word processor program. That file was sent into an Apple Macintosh™ system by Gary & Linda Duarte of DeskTop ComPosition Systems, Inc. Reno, NV where it was typesetter formatted with a program called Stylo-Type I™. This program can process direct Linotronic typesetter commands not requiring PostScript™. The final edited version of the book was then output through a Linotronic 300 typesetting system by Reno Typographers. Text type is Times Roman, display type is Franklin Gothic. The front and back cover text and graphics were done by DeskTop ComPosition Systems Inc. with the Macintosh SE™ and the Aldus PageMaker™ program.

The printing was done by Braun Brumfield, Inc. Ann Arbor, MI on 60 lb white offset paper stock and 10 point CIS Frankote cover stock.